The Voice

GW01466487

Emma Seiler

(Translator: William Henry Furness)

Alpha Editions

This edition published in 2024

ISBN : 9789362995667

Design and Setting By
Alpha Editions
www.alphaedis.com
Email - info@alphaedis.com

Contents

TRANSLATOR'S PREFACE

THE translator of this book, desirous, in common with other friends of its author, that her claims as a lady of rare scientific attainments should be recognized in this country, where she has recently taken up her abode, has obtained her consent to the publication of the following testimonials to her position in her own country from gentlemen of the highest eminence in science:

[TRANSLATED]

MAD. EMMA SEILER has dwelt for a long time here in Heidelberg, and given instruction in singing. She has won the reputation of a very careful, skilled and learned teacher, possessing a fine ear and cultivated taste. While engaged on my book, "*Die Lehre von den Tonempfindungen, &c.*," I had the honor of becoming acquainted with Mad. Seiler, and of being assisted by her in my essay upon the formation of the vowel tones and the registers of the female voice. I have thus had an opportunity of knowing the delicacy of her musical ear and her ability to master the more difficult and abstract parts of the theory of music.

I have pleasure in bearing this testimony to her worth, in the hope of securing for her the confidence and the encouragement of those who are interested in the scientific culture of music, and who know how desirable it is that an instructress in the art of singing should be possessed of scientific knowledge, a fine ear, and a cultivated taste.

(Signed) DR. H. HELMHOLTZ,

Prof. of Physiology, Member of the Academies and Royal Societies of London, Edinburgh, Amsterdam, Stockholm, Berlin, Vienna, Munich, Göttingen.

HEIDELBERG, Aug. 5, 1866

[TRANSLATED]

MAD. E. SEILER has made for herself an honorable name in Germany, not only as a practical teacher of singing, but also by her valuable investigations in regard to the culture of the musical voice. By her own anatomical studies she has acquired a thorough knowledge of the vocal organs, and by means of the laryngoscope has advanced, in the way first trodden by Garcia, to the establishment of the conditions of the formation of the voice. We owe to her a more exact knowledge of the position of the larynx, and of its parts in the production of the several registers of the human voice; and she appears especially to have brought to a final and satisfactory decision the much-vexed question respecting the formation of the so-called *fistel tones* (head tones). She has been associated with the best powers possessed by Germany in the department of the theory of music and physiological acoustics, standing by the side of the celebrated physiologist, Helmholtz, while he was engaged in his physiologico-acoustic work upon the generation of the vowels and the nature of harmony.

(Signed) E. DU BOIS-REYMOND,

Professor of Physiology in the Royal University of Berlin.

BERLIN, July 17, 1866

In a letter, written in English, addressed to the President and Members of the American Philosophical Society, Professor du Bois-Reymond introduces Mrs. Seiler (italicizing the words) *"as a lady of truly remarkable scientific attainments."* "Prompted," he states, "by a spirit of philosophical inquiry, not frequently met with in her sex, she has made herself entirely acquainted with all the facts and theories concerning the production of the human voice. She has entered, deeper probably than any one else before her, into the study of the problem of the different registers of the human voice. Most of her results she has published in a pamphlet under the title: *Altes und Neues über die Ausbildung des Gesangorganes* (Leipzig, 1861), which has received the approbation of both the physiologists and the singing masters of this country."

The translator takes the opportunity to state that, as he makes no pretensions to any knowledge either of the science or of the art of music, his translation has been carefully revised by persons entirely competent to correct its musical phraseology.

W. H. F.

PHILADELPHIA, December, 1867.

INTRODUCTION

IN giving to the public these fruits of years of earnest labor, and in attempting to bring into harmony things which have always been treated separately, the Science and the Art of Singing, it seems necessary that I should state the reasons that prompted me to this study.

As I had for many years the advantage of the best tuition, both German and Italian, in the Art of Singing, and had often sung with favor in concerts, I was led to believe myself qualified to become a teacher of this art. But hardly had I undertaken the office before I felt that, while I was able to teach my pupils to execute pieces of music with tolerable accuracy and with the appropriate expression, I was wanting in the knowledge of any sure starting-point, any sound principle, from which to proceed in the special culture of any individual voice. In order to obtain the knowledge which thus appeared to be requisite in a teacher of vocal music, I examined the best schools of singing; and when I learned nothing from them that I did not already know, I sought the most celebrated teachers of singing to learn what was wanting. But what one teacher announced to me as a rule was usually rejected by another. Every teacher had his own peculiar system of instruction. No one could give me any definite reasons therefor, and the best assured me that so exact a method as I sought did not exist, and that every teacher must find his own way through his own experience. In such a state of darkness and uncertainty, to undertake to instruct others appeared to me a manifest wrong, for in no branch of instruction can the ignorance of the teacher do greater injury than in the teaching of vocal music. This I unhappily learned from my own personal experience, when, under the tuition of a most eminent teacher, I entirely lost my voice, whereby the embarrassment I was under, so far from being diminished, was only increased. After this misfortune I studied under *Frederick Wiek*, in Dresden (the father and instructor of Clara Schumann), in order to become a teacher on the piano. But while I thus devoted myself to this branch of teaching exclusively, it became from that time the aim and effort of my life to obtain such a knowledge of the human voice as is indispensable to a natural and healthy development of its beautiful powers.

I availed myself of every opportunity to hear Jenny Lind, who was then dwelling in Dresden, and to learn all that I could from her. I likewise hoped, by a protracted abode in Italy, the land of song, to attain the fulfilment of my wishes; but, beyond certain practical advantages, I gathered there no sure and radical knowledge. In the French method of instruction, now so popular, I found the same superficiality and uncertainty that existed everywhere else. But the more deeply I was impressed with this state of things, and the more fully I became aware of the injurious and trying consequences of the method of teaching followed at the present day, the more earnestly was I impelled to press onward in search of light and clearness in this dim domain.

Convinced that only by the way of scientific investigation the desired end could be reached, I sought the counsel of Prof. *Helmholtz*, in Heidelberg. This distinguished man was then engaged in a scientific inquiry into the natural laws lying at the basis of musical sounds. Prof. Helmholtz permitted me to take part in his investigations, and at his kind suggestion I attempted by myself, by means of the laryngoscope, to observe the physiological processes that go on in the larynx during the production of different tones. My special thanks are due to him that now, with a more thorough knowledge of the human voice, I can give instruction in singing without the fear of doing any injury. My thanks are due in a like manner to Prof. *du Bois-Reymond*, in Berlin, who, at a later period, also gave me his friendly help in my studies.

In 1861 I published a part of my investigations in Germany, where they found acknowledgment and favor. That little work is contained in the following pages, together with some account of the discoveries of Professor *Helmholtz* relating to the human voice, and of their practical application to the education of the voice in singing.

The practical sense of the American people enables them, above all others, to appreciate the worth of every discovery and of every advance. And therefore it is my earnest hope that the publication of these investigations in this country may help to elevate and improve the Art of Singing.

I
VOCAL MUSIC
ITS RISE, DEVELOPMENT AND DECLINE

IT is a matter of complaint among all persons of good taste, who take an intelligent interest in art, and especially in music, that fine singers are becoming more and more rare, while formerly there appears never to have been any lack of men and women eminent in this art. The complaint seems not altogether without reason, when we revert to that rich summer-time of song, not yet lying very far behind us, in the last half of the last century, and compare it with the present. The retrospect shows us plainly that the art of singing has descended from its former high estate, and is now in a condition of decline. When we consider what is told us in the historical works of *Forkel, Burney, Kiesewetter, Brendel* and others, and compare it with our present poverty in good voices and skilful artists, we are struck with the multitude of fine voices then heard, with their remarkable fulness of tone, as well as with the considerable number of singers—male and female—appearing at the same time.

We first recall to mind the last great artists of that time, whose names are familiar to us because they appeared in public after the beginning of the present century:—*Catalani*, who preserved to extreme old age the melody and enormous power of her voice; *Malibran, Sontag, Vespermann,* &c.; the men singers, *Rubini, Tamburini, Lablache,* and others; and, still farther back, *Mara,* whose voice had a compass, with equal fulness of tone, of three octaves, and who possessed such a power of musical utterance that she imitated within the compass of her voice the most difficult passages of the violin and flute with perfect facility. Then comes the artiste *Ajugara Bastardella*, in Parma, who executed with purity and distinctness the most difficult passages from si

to si , and roulades with successive trills, with enchanting harmony; and the old Italian singing-masters, who sang and taught with an art which we should scarcely hold possible, were it not for the unanimous testimony of their contemporaries. There were *Porpora* and his pupil *Perugia*, who sang two full octaves, with successive trills up and down in one breath, and executed with perfect exactness all the tones of the chromatic scale without an accompaniment; and *Farinelli*, who to his latest age preserved his wonderfully beautiful voice. Of him it is related, among other things, that on one occasion he competed with a trumpeter, who accompanied him in an aria. After both had several times dwelt on notes in which each sought to excel the other in power and duration, they prolonged a note with a double trill in thirds, which they continued until both seemed to be exhausted. At last the trumpeter gave up, entirely out of breath, while Farinelli, without taking breath, prolonged the note with renewed volume of sound, trilling and ending, finally, with the most difficult of roulades. *Pistochi* and *Bernucchi* rivalled Farinelli. The latter, although he had received from nature a refractory voice of little excellence, nevertheless succeeded in cultivating it so highly that he became one of the most distinguished artists of his day, called by Händel and Graun, "The King of Singers."

It is impossible to mention by name all the many singers, male and female, who won applause and renown in the beginning and in the middle of the last century. Almost every European state was furnished with most excellent operas, and troops of artists, men and women, with voices of the highest cultivation, flocked thither. Even in the streets and inns and other places in Italy, where elsewhere we are accustomed to seek only music of the lowest kind, one could then hear the most artistic vocal music, such as was found in the churches, concert-saloons and theatres of Germany and France.

It appears that far greater demands were made upon singers then than now-a-days. At least, history celebrates, together with the great vocal flexibility of the earlier singers, the measured beauty of their singing, the noble tone, the thoroughly cultivated delivery, by which they showed themselves true artists, and produced upon their hearers effects almost miraculous.

On the other hand, how sad is the condition of vocal music in our time! How few artistically cultivated voices are there! And the few that there are, how soon are they used up and lost! Artists like *Lind*, and more recently *Trebelli*, are exceptions to be made.

Mediocre talent is now often sought, and rewarded far beyond its desert. One is often tempted to think that the public at large has wellnigh lost all capacity of judgment, when he witnesses the representation of one of our operas. Let a singer, male or female, only drawl the notes sentimentally one into another, execute a tremulo upon prolonged notes, introduce very often the softest piano and just where it is entirely out of place, growl out the lowest notes in the roughest timbre, and scream out the high notes lustily, and he or she may reckon with certainty upon the greatest applause. In fact, we have become so easily pleased that even an impure execution is suffered to pass without comment. Let the personal appearance of the singer only be handsome and prepossessing, he need trouble himself little about his art in order to win the favor of the public. This decline of the art of singing is usually ascribed to the want of good voices, and this poverty of voices to our altered modes of living. To me it appears as the natural consequence of the whole manner and way in which the art of singing has been historically developed since its earlier high state of perfection.

The human voice is, of all instruments, the most natural, the most perfect, the most intimate in its relation to us, as, for the use of it, we have a talent or faculty innate, which, in the case of other instruments, can only be laboriously acquired, to say nothing of the fact that these instruments are first to be invented and put together. Hence vocal music appears to have been almost the only music among the Greeks, and the rude instruments then in use served merely for an accompaniment. The history of our so-called *Western* music, which dates no farther back than the fourth century after Christ, tells us hardly anything else than of vocal musicians and of their compositions for concerted and chorus singing.

Our art, only slowly developing itself from those earliest times, was cherished, mainly in Italy, for the sole purpose of exalting divine worship. We have, at least, no account of any secular art of music in those days. As yet unacquainted with harmony, the only singing was *in unison*, as was the custom, at an earlier period, among the Greeks; for not until the tenth century of the Christian era was it attempted, and then by a Flemish monk (*Hukbaldus*), to harmonize several and different notes; thus was invented and founded our harmony, whose exponent was the organ.⊥

From that time forward, history makes mention of many persons who labored worthily, now more and now less, to create a theory of music, seeking to found a system of harmony upon that rude beginning, and by degrees to improve it. In the fourteenth and fifteenth centuries music burst forth into blossom in the Netherlands, and thenceforth rose steadily in excellence, when also it began to branch out into the excesses of counterpoint. The fame of the Netherlands soon spread over all the civilized countries of Europe. The artists of the Netherlands were invited upon the most favorable terms to Italy, France, Spain, and Germany, and thus the progress of music spread over all these countries almost *pari passu*. For two hundred years the Netherlands maintained the reputation of the best and highest culture in vocal music, and not until the middle of the sixteenth century did there appear in Italy and Germany artists who attained to a like renown. Up to that time prejudice denied to the Italians *all talent for music*, as it has ever since exaggerated their claims in this respect. *Kiesewetter* remarks, in his History of Music, that, although the Netherlands in Italy no longer had the monopoly, they nevertheless always maintained the supremacy in music. Climate and language were, however, so favorable to vocal music in Italy that it soon found there its peculiar home, and though theoretical knowledge of music was advanced by the earlier singers, now richness and power of voice were also attained. As it had previously been with the Netherlanders, so it now became with the Italians. They were drawn to all countries in which there was any love of art; and they soon won that supremacy in music which they maintained until the last century. Until the latter part of the sixteenth century, good musicians were devoted almost exclusively to church music, and held it beneath their dignity to take part in music of any other kind. All but church music they left to the minstrels and strolling singers, who traveled over the country from place to place, and in different lands were styled *minstrels*, *minnesänger* and *trovatori*. They mostly sung love-songs, which they often extemporized in word and tune, finding place and popularity on all festive occasions. But under the impulse which music began to feel, the desire among the educated class to revive the old Greek drama, which just at that period had come to be well known, became more and more urgent. Imbued with the spirit of that age, the whole tendency of which was to exalt the ancient classic poets, a circle of men of science and culture from the higher classes gave themselves to the task of producing a style of music such as the Greeks must have had in the representation of their dramas. In the mansion of Count *Bardi*, in Florence, then the centre of union for all who had any claims to cultivation, music was first arranged for a *single* voice by a dilettante, the father of the renowned Galileo.

This attempt met with applause and imitation among the most distinguished singers of the time, who thenceforth turned their attention also to secular music. It thus came about that, towards the end of the sixteenth century, on festal occasions in Italy, and even earlier in France, theatrical representations were given with vocal music. This music was, however, always composed in the form of the chorus, and the leading voice alone was represented by a singer; the other voices were represented by instruments.

Such was the beginning of solo singing, which, growing ever more in public favor, soon came to be introduced into the most solemn church music; dramatic representations, religious and secular, grew very popular, and were the forerunners of the opera and oratorio, the richest inventions of the sixteenth century.

Up to this time, a singer of sound musical culture sufficed for chorus singing, but by the introduction of solo singing a more complete education of the organ of singing became a necessity. Indeed, as early as the middle of the fifteenth century there existed in Rome and Milan schools of music and professorships for the education of singers; but with the introduction and diffusion of solo singing similar conservatories were established in nearly all the more considerable cities of Italy, and all the energies of the musician were devoted to the highest possible culture of the voice.

But, with solo singing, greater attention was paid to instruments, which were already in those days constructed with the greatest care and skill. With the higher cultivation of single voices, chorus singing also became richer in harmony and embellishment, but as, in vocal music, words accompany the music, the expression of the music becomes more definite and intelligible for the hearer, and thus with the higher cultivation of vocal music, and by means of it, even our whole modern system of harmony has been developed.

Women were, by ecclesiastical law, excluded from participation in church music, and as the voices of boys could be used only for a few years, they did not suffice to meet the ever-increasing demands of church music. At first it was attempted to supply the place of the sopranists and contraltists with so-called falsettists. As, however, these substitutes proved insufficient, the soprano and contralto of boys were sought to be preserved in men. And so, in 1625, appeared the first male sopranist in the Papal chapel in Rome. Such sopranists and contraltists soon appeared in great numbers, and as their organs of singing continued soft and tender as those of women, and their compass was the same, to them the education of female voices was given over exclusively. Thenceforth women became the richest ornament of the opera, then blooming into beauty. But only when the ecclesiastical law forbidding women to take part in church music was annulled, did women begin, in the middle of the last century, to take the place of those male sopranists and contraltists.

It thus became unnecessary to secure longer duration to the voices of boys, especially as these were never able to attain to the peculiar grace of the female voice, and so this class of singers gradually died out. But still in the first half of the present century there were many of them living and sought for as teachers of singing. *To the disappearance of this kind of singers, Rossini thinks the decline of vocal art is to be mainly ascribed.*

The art of singing rose in the course of the seventeenth century to an extraordinary height of cultivation, and was diffused more and more by means of the opera, then blooming, as we have said, into beauty. But in that brilliant springtime of vocal art, it was not mere externals, such as beauty of tone, flexibility, etc., that were striven for, but, above all, the correct expression of the feeling intended in the composition. This rendered necessary to the singer the most thorough æsthetic culture, going hand in hand with the culture of the vocal organ. For only thus could he succeed in acting upon the souls of his hearers, in moving them and carrying them along with him in the emotions which the music awakened in his own mind. The dramatic singer was now strongly tempted to neglect the externals of his art for the æsthetic, purely inward conception of the music. Certain, at least, it is that to the neglect of the training of the voice (*Tonbildung*), and to the style of writing of our modern composers—a style unsuited to the art of singing, and looking only to its spiritual element—the decline of this art is in part to be traced. *Mannstein* says that, with the disappearance of those great masters, power and beauty of tone have fallen more and more into contempt, and at the present day it is scarcely known what is meant by them. True it is, that a beautiful tone of voice (*Gesangston*), which must be considered the foundation and first requisition of fine singing, is more and more rare among our singers, male and female, and yet it is just as important in music as perfect form in the creations of the sculptor.

But the complete technical education of the earlier singers misled many of them into various unnatural artifices, in order to obtain notice and distinction. The applause of the public caused such trickeries to become the fashion among artists. The multitude, accustomed to such effects, began to mistake them for art. By the gradual disappearance of the male sopranists, instruction in singing fell into the hands of tenor singers, who usually cultivated the female voice in accordance with their own voices, which could not be otherwise than injurious in the uncertainty existing as to the limits in compass and the difference between the male and female organs of voice.

Thus it has come to pass that people are now apt to imagine that they know all that is to be known; and as teaching in singing is generally best paid, the office has been undertaken, without the slightest apparent self-distrust, by many persons who have not the slightest idea what thorough acquaintance with the organs of singing, what comprehensive knowledge of all the departments of music and what æsthetic and general culture, the teacher of singing requires. Very few persons indeed clearly understand what is meant by the education of a voice, and what high qualifications both teacher and pupil always require. The idea, for instance, is very prevalent that every musician, whatever may be the branch of music to which he is devoted, and especially every singer, is qualified to give instruction in singing. And therefore a dilettanteism without precedent has taken the place of all real artistic endeavors. Be this, however, as it may, such is the wide diffusion and popularity of music beyond all the other arts, that the want of singers artistically educated, and consequently also of a recognized sound method of instruction, becomes more and more urgent; and although we have in these times distinguished singers, male and female, as well as skilful teachers, yet the number is very small and by no means equal to the demand.

But now, as every evil, as soon as it is felt to be such, calls forth the means of its removal, already in various ways attempts are making in the department of the Art of Singing to restore it as perfectly as possible to its former high position, and if possible to elevate it to a yet higher state. It was natural that the attempt should, first of all, be made to revive the old Italian method of instruction, and that, by strict adherence in everything to what has come down to us by tradition, we should hope for deliverance and salvation; for to the Italians mainly vocal music was indebted for its chief glory. Without considering in what a sadly superficial way music—and vocal music especially—is now treated in Italy, many have given in to the erroneous idea that any Italian who can sing anything must know how to educate a voice. Thus many incompetent Italians have become popular teachers in other countries.

The old Italian method of instruction, to which vocal music owed its high condition, was purely *empirical*, i. e., the old singing masters taught only according to a sound and just feeling for the beautiful, guided by that faculty of acute observation, which enabled them to distinguish what belongs to nature. Their pupils learned by imitation, as children learn their mother tongue, without troubling themselves about rules. But after the true and natural way has once been forsaken, and for so long a period only the false and the unnatural has been heard and taught, it seems almost impossible by empiricism alone to restore the old and proper method of teaching. With our higher degree of culture, men and things have greatly changed. Our feeling is no longer sufficiently simple and natural to distinguish the true without the help of scientific principles.

But science has already done much to assist the formation of musical forms of art. Mathematics and physics have established the principal laws of sound and the processes of sound, in accordance with which our musical instruments are now constructed. Philosophical inquirers have succeeded also in discovering the eternal and impregnable laws of Nature upon which the mutual influences of melody, harmony and rhythm depend, and in thus giving to composition fixed forms and laws which no one ventures to question. And more recently Professor Helmholtz, in his great work, "*Die Lehre von den Tonempfindungen*," has given to music of all kinds a scientific ground and basis. But for the culture of the human voice in singing science has as yet furnished only a few lights. The well-known experiments of *Johannes Müller* upon the larynx gave us all that was known, until very recently, respecting the functions of the organ of singing. Many singing masters have sought to found their methods of instruction upon these observations on the larynx, at the same time putting forth the boldest conjectures in regard to the functions of the organ of singing in the living subject. But they have thus ruined more fine voices than those teachers who, without reference to the formation of the voice, only correct the musical faults of their pupils, and for the rest let them sing as they please.

This superficial treatment of science, and the unfortunate results of its application, have injured the art of singing more than benefited it, and created a prejudice against all scientific investigations in this direction among the most distinguished artists and teachers, as well as among those who take an intelligent interest in this department of music. It is a pretty common opinion that science can do little for the improvement of music, and nothing for the culture and preservation of the voice in singing. And the habit of regarding science and art as opposed to each other renders it extremely difficult to secure a hearing for the results of thorough scientific inquiry in this direction.

Science itself admits that it can neither create artistic talent, nor supply the place of it, but only furnish it with aids. Besides, with the whole inner nature of music, no forms of thought (*reflection*) have anything to do. It has "a reason above reason." This art transmits to us in sound the expression of emotions as they rise in the human soul and connect themselves one with another. It is the revelation of our inmost life in its tenderest and finest processes, and is therefore the most ideal of the arts. It appeals directly to our consciousness. As a sense of the divine dwells in every nation, in every human being, and is impelled to form for itself a religious cultus, so we find among all nations the need of music dwelling as deeply in human nature. The most uncivilized tribes celebrate their festivals with songs as the expression of their devotion or joy, and the cultivated nations of ancient times, like the Greeks, cherished music as the ethereal vehicle of their poetry, and regarded it as the chief aid in the culture of the soul.

But together with its purely internal character, music has yet another and formal side, for if our art consisted only in the æsthetic feeling, and in representing this feeling, every person of culture, possessing the right feeling, would be able to sing, just as he understands how to read intelligibly.

Everything spiritual, everything ideal, as soon as it is to be made present to the perceptions of others, requires a form which, in its material as well as in its structure, may be more or less perfect, but it can never otherwise than submit to those eternal laws to which all that lives, all that comes within the sphere of our perceptions, is subject. To discover and establish the natural laws which lie at the basis of all our forms of art is the office of science; to fashion and control these forms and animate them with a soul is the task of art. In singing, the art consists in tones beautiful and sonorous, and fitted for the expression of every variation of feeling. To set forth the natural laws by which these tones are produced is the business of physiology and physics.

Thus is there not only an *æsthetical* side to the art of singing, but a *physiological* and a *physical* side also, without an exact knowledge, appreciation, observance, and study of which, what is hurtful cannot be discerned and avoided; and no true culture of art, and consequently no progress in singing, is possible.

In the *physiological* view of vocal art, we have to do with the quality and strength of the organ of singing in the act of uttering sound, and under the variations of sound that take place in certain tones (the register being transcended).

By the *physical* side is to be understood the correct use and skilful management of the air flowing from the lungs through the windpipe, and brought into vibration by the vocal chords in the larynx.

But the *æsthetics* of vocal art, and the spiritual inspiration of the form (of the sound), comprise the whole domain of music and poetic beauty.

---

1 Those who are interested in the history of music are referred to the historical works already mentioned for a fuller account of what is only alluded to above.

II
PHYSIOLOGICAL VIEW
FORMATION OF SOUND BY THE ORGAN OF THE HUMAN VOICE

THE great physiologist, Johannes Müller, fastened a larynx, which he had cut out with the whole trachea belonging to it, to a board, and, stretching the vocal chords by a weight that could be increased or diminished at pleasure, caused vibrations in it by blowing through the trachea with a pair of bellows, or through a tube with his own breath. In this way he succeeded in producing almost all the tones of the human voice, and even some which are beyond the compass of this organ.

He distinguished two different kinds of tones, to which he gave the names of the chest register and the falsetto register. The chest tones were produced when the vocal ligaments, slackly stretched, were made to vibrate easily in their whole breadth; the falsetto tones came merely through the vibration of the fine inner edges of the vocal chords when they were more tightly stretched. At a moderate stretching of the vocal chords, it depended upon the manner of blowing whether a sound corresponding to the chest voice or to the falsetto were produced, or whether it were higher or lower for several tones, often for a whole octave. A series of tones of more than two octaves could thus be produced in the same larynx, with, however, gaps and places at which the vocal chords, instead of being stretched gradually, have to be *stretched at once very strongly, in order that the succeeding higher half tone may be reached.*

Such a place Müller indicates from c² to c#2, or d² to d#2

, with the remark that it differs in different larynxes, being in some higher and in some lower. But in order to render practicable the proper stretching of the exsected larynx, muscles and membranes have to be cut, which sufficiently proves that the functions of the organ of singing in the living must be differently carried on.

Dr. Merkel, in Leipzig, has continued these experiments, and by means of a peculiar contrivance has succeeded in producing all the tones in the exsected larynx, without mutilating it. But these investigations, interesting as they are, throw no certain light upon the formation of sound by the vocal organ in the living.

The celebrated singing master, *Manuel Garcia,* now living in London, was the first to adopt the right mode of scientific inquiry in this department, with favorable results. He undertook to apply the laryngoscope (previously invented by the Englishman, *Liston*) to the larynx in the act of singing. The interesting results of these observations were published by him in the *Philosophical Mag. and Journal of Science*, vol. x. p. 218. While men of science immediately repeated Garcia's experiments and applied them with the greatest advantage to pathological purposes, they were received with distrust, scarcely noticed, and in many instances entirely rejected, by teachers of vocal music. The few who attempted to follow the path thus opened soon gave it up, because they lacked either patience or the anatomical knowledge necessary to such investigations.

The laryngoscope is well known among medical men. It is a small plane mirror of glass or metal, having a long handle. Before it is introduced into the throat, it is first warmed, to prevent its becoming dimmed. The reflecting surface of this instrument is directed downwards and forwards, so that it receives the reflection caught from a concave mirror, and presents to the eye of the observer a picture of the illuminated larynx. In using it upon oneself, there is need of a second mirror, which must be so held that the image may be seen in the laryngoscope.

The use of the laryngoscope requires in the observer a certain adroitness and long-continued practice—almost more in the observer than in the subject of observation. In self-observation one must first learn to overcome the irritation always caused at the first by the contact of the mirror with the back of the throat. Once accustomed to the contact, one soon succeeds in obtaining a sight of the larynx, sufficient for the most part for pathological purposes. But it requires long practice before one can control those organs, usually not immediately submissive to the will, and raise the epiglottis, so as to be able to see into the whole larynx. But this is absolutely indispensable, in the observation of the formation of sound, to the attainment of any substantial results. Garcia says himself that *one-third of the glottis* was always *hidden* from him by the epiglottis, and to this circumstance is the unsatisfactory character of his observations to be ascribed. But even when, after long practice, one is able at last to bring the whole glottis into view, this is not by any means enough. Not until observation has been so long continued that all the movements of the vocal organ are normal, notwithstanding the unnatural drawing back of the epiglottis, and not until the process that goes on is found again and again to be always the same, can it be recognized as fact.

As Garcia is the most eminent of singing masters now living, and as he has sought, solely in the interest of vocal music, to ascertain the mechanism by which sound is formed, and as his observations have been confirmed by men of science, I give them here in his own words.

In order that what follows may be better understood by those unacquainted with anatomy, a brief anatomical description of the vocal organ will be found in an Appendix to the present work.

OBSERVATIONS WITH THE LARYNGOSCOPE
BY MANUEL GARCIA

"At the moment when the person draws a deep breath, the epiglottis being raised, we are able to see the following series of movements: the arytenoid cartilages become separated by a very free lateral movement; the superior ligaments are placed against the ventricles; the inferior ligaments are also drawn back, though in a less degree, into the same cavities; and the glottis, large and wide open, is exhibited, so as to show in part the rings of the trachea. But, unfortunately, however dexterous we may be in disposing these organs, and even when we are most successful, at least *the third part of the anterior of the glottis remains concealed by the epiglottis.*

"As soon as we prepare to produce a sound, the arytenoid cartilages approach each other, and press together by their interior surfaces, and by their anterior apophyses, without leaving any space, or inter-cartilaginous glottis; sometimes, even, they come in contact so closely as to cross each other by the tubercles of Santorini. To this movement of the anterior apophyses that of the ligaments of the glottis corresponds, which detach themselves from the ventricles, come in contact with different degrees of energy, and show themselves at the bottom of the larynx, under the form of an ellipse of a yellowish color. The superior ligaments, together with the aryteno-epiglottidean folds, assist to form the tube which surmounts the glottis; and being the lower and free extremity of that tube, enframe the ellipse, the surface of which they enlarge or diminish according as they enter more or less into the ventricles. These last scarcely retain a trace of their opening. By anticipation, we might say of these cavities that, as will afterwards appear clearly enough in these pages, they only afford to the two pair of ligaments a space in which they may easily range themselves. When the aryteno-epiglottidean folds contract, they lower the epiglottis and make the superior orifice of the larynx considerably narrower.

"The meeting of the lips of the glottis, naturally proceeding from the front towards the back, if this movement is well managed, will allow, between the apophyses, *of the formation of a triangular space or inter-cartilaginous glottis*, but one which, however, is closed as soon as the sounds are produced.

"After some essays we perceive that this internal disposition of the larynx is only visible when the epiglottis remains raised. But neither all the registers of the voice, nor all the degrees of intensity, are equally fitted for its taking this position. We soon discover that the brilliant and powerful sounds of the chest register contract the cavity of the larynx, and close still more its orifice; and, on the contrary, that veiled notes, and notes of moderate power, open both, so as to render any observation easy. The falsetto register especially possesses this prerogative, as well as the first notes of the head voice. So as to render these facts more precise, we will study in the voice of the tenor the ascending progression of the chest register, and in the soprano that of the falsetto and head registers.

EMISSION OF THE CHEST VOICE

"If we emit veiled and feeble sounds, the larynx opens at the notes

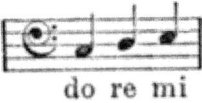

do re mi , and we see the glottis agitated by large and loose vibrations throughout its entire extent. Its lips comprehend in their length the anterior apophyses of the arytenoid cartilages and the vocal chords; but, I repeat it, there remains no triangular space.

"As the sounds ascend, the apophyses, which are slightly rounded on their internal side, by a gradual apposition commencing at the back encroach on

si do

the length of the glottis, and as soon as we reach the sounds they finish by touching each other throughout their whole extent; but their summits are only solidly fixed one against the other at the notes

do re . In some organs these summits are a little vacillating when they form the posterior end of the glottis, and two or three half-tones which are formed show a certain want of purity and strength, which is very well

known to singers. From do re the vibrations, having become rounder and purer, are accomplished by *the vocal ligaments alone,* up to the end of the register.

"The glottis at this moment presents the aspect of a line slightly swelled towards its middle, the length of which diminishes still more as the voice ascends. We also see that the cavity of the larynx has become very small, and that the superior ligaments have contracted the extent of the ellipse to less than one-half.

"Thus the organs act with a double difference: 1. The cavity of the larynx contracts itself more when the voice is intense than when it is feeble. 2. The superior ligaments are contracted, so as to reduce the small diameter of the ellipse to a width of two or three lines. But however powerful these contractions may be, neither the cartilages of Wrisberg, nor the superior ligaments themselves, ever close sufficiently to prevent the passage of the air, or even to render it difficult. This fact, which is verified also with regard to the falsetto and head registers, suffices to prove that the superior ligaments do not fill a generative part in the formation of the voice. We may draw the same conclusion by considering the position occupied by the somewhat feeble muscles which correspond to these ligaments; they cover externally the extremity of the diverging fibres of the thyro-arytenoid muscles, and take part especially in the contractions of the cavity of the larynx during the formation of the high notes of the chest and head registers.

PRODUCTION OF THE FALSETTO

"The low notes of the falsetto show the glottis infinitely better than the unisons of the chest voice, and produce vibrations more extended and more distinct. Its vibrating sides, formed by the anterior apophyses of the arytenoid cartilages and by the ligaments, become gradually shorter as the voice

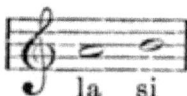

ascends; at the notes **la si** the apophyses take part only at their summits; and in these notes there results a weakness similar to that which we have remarked in the chest notes an octave below. At the notes

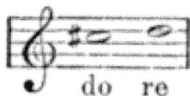

do re, the ligaments alone continue to act; then begins the series of notes called the *head voice*. The moment in which the action of the apophyses ceases exhibits in the female voice a very sensible difference to the ear and in the organ itself. Lastly, we verify that up to the highest sounds of the register the glottis continues to diminish in length and in width.

"If we compare the two registers in these movements, we shall find some analogies in them; the sides of the glottis formed at first by the apophyses and the ligaments become shorter by degrees, and end by consisting only of the ligaments. The chest register is divided into two parts, corresponding to these two states of the glottis. The register of falsetto-head presents a complete similarity, and in a still more striking manner.

"On other points, on the contrary, these same registers are very unlike. The length of the glottis necessary to form a falsetto note always exceeds that which produces the unison of the chest. The movements which agitate the sides of the glottis are also augmented, and keep the vibrating orifice continually half opened, which naturally produces a great waste of air. A last trait of difference is in the increased extent of that elliptic surface.

"All these circumstances show in the mechanism of the falsetto a state of relaxation which we do not find in the same degree in the chest register.

MANNER IN WHICH THE SOUNDS ARE FORMED

"As we have just seen—and what we have seen proves it—the inferior ligaments at the bottom of the larynx form exclusively the voice, whatever may be its register or its intensity; for they alone vibrate at the bottom of the larynx.... By the compressions and expansions of the air, or the successive and regular explosions which it produces in passing through the glottis, sound is produced." (*The London, Edinburgh and Dublin Phil. Mag. and Journal of Science*, vol. x. 4th Series, pp. 218–221, 1855.)

Garcia proceeds, in the same paper, to give an elaborate account of his theory of the compression, expansion and explosion of the air in expiration, together with his conjectures as to the action of the muscles of the larynx in relation to the different registers. I omit both here, for, since this publication of Garcia's, the movements of the breath generating sound in expiration have been thoroughly investigated and determined by Prof. Helmholtz; and in the physical section of the present work all may be found that is of value in the culture of the singing voice. Whatever can be definitely communicated in regard to the working of the muscles of the larynx may likewise be found in any anatomical work. An acquaintance, however, with the action of these muscles is not directly necessary to our purpose, and is of interest only to the physiologist.

It is not to be denied that Garcia's observations do not, by any means, lead to satisfactory conclusions as to the functions of the vocal organ. He has, as we shall see in the sequel, attached special importance to much that is unessential and abnormal, and the main facts, the elucidation of which is particularly needed, he has scarcely mentioned. Thus he tells us nothing of that series of tones which he calls the head register. The transition also of the registers he has not carefully examined and observed in different voices: the chest register in the male and the falsetto of the female voice.

Nevertheless, these investigations possess much that is valuable, and are of special value to the art of singing, because they teach a method hitherto unknown of observing the larynx, by which sure and satisfactory results are reached. And when an acquaintance with these results comes to be universally diffused, and the art of singing is thereby led into the right direction, we shall owe it most especially to the excellent experimental observations of Garcia.

Garcia has accepted the division made by Müller, and universally adopted in science, of the chest, falsetto and head registers. I employ the same distinctions—a fact which it seems worth while to mention, simply because every teacher and school have their own terminology, and instead of falsetto we have *fistel*, *throat*, and *middle* or *neck* voice, &c. These denominations of the same registers have thus far only increased the obscurity prevailing in the art of singing.

MY OWN OBSERVATIONS WITH THE LARYNGOSCOPE

In giving an account of my own observations with the laryngoscope, I premise that laryngoscopy has of late attracted much attention among the learned, and that *Czermak, Turk, Merkel, Lewin, Bataille,* &c., have published a series of valuable observations, all of which, however, with the exception of Bataille's, were made in the interest of science, for pathological purposes especially. My aim, in the employment of the laryngoscope, has been directed exclusively to the discovery of the natural limits of the different registers of the human voice; and although I have thus been able to observe many other interesting processes, it would not at all accord with the design of this book to communicate observations which have no direct relation to the culture of the voice in singing, and which come better from men of science than from a teacher of vocal music.

In using the laryngoscope while the breath is quietly drawn, I saw, as Garcia did, the whole larynx wide open, so that one could easily introduce a finger into it, and the rings of the trachea were plainly visible.

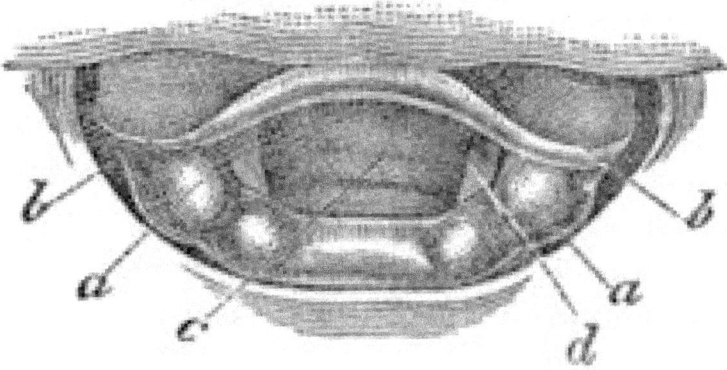

a. Arytenoid cartilages.

b. Epiglottis.

c. Trachea.[2]

d. Vocal chords.

When those who had become accustomed to the introduction of the instrument sang, at my request, *a,* as pronounced in the English word *man,* in a deep tone, the epiglottis rose, the tongue formed a cavity from within forwards, and thus rendered it easy to see into the larynx. So soon as the *a,* as in *father,* was sung, the cover quickly fell, the tongue rose, and prevented all observation of the organ of singing. The other vowels are still less favorable to observation, because they do not admit of any such wide opening of the mouth. Strong tones also are unfavorable to observation, as Garcia also remarked; and this is very natural, because strong and sonorous tones require greater exertions of the singing organ, and, above all things, the right position of those parts of the larynx and mouth which serve as a resonance apparatus in the formation of sound. In order to be able to see perfectly the whole glottis, all this resonance apparatus must be drawn back as far as possible, and the rim of the larynx must be tolerably flat. Thus only faint and weak sounds are favorable to observation.

THE CHEST REGISTER

When the vowel *a,* as in *man,* was sung, I could, after long-continued practice, plainly see how the arytenoid cartilages quickly rose with their summits in their mucous membranous case and approached to mutual contact. In like manner, the *chordæ vocales,* or inferior vocal chords, approached each other so closely that scarcely any space between them was observable. The superior or false vocal ligaments formed the ellipse described by Garcia in the upper part of the glottis.

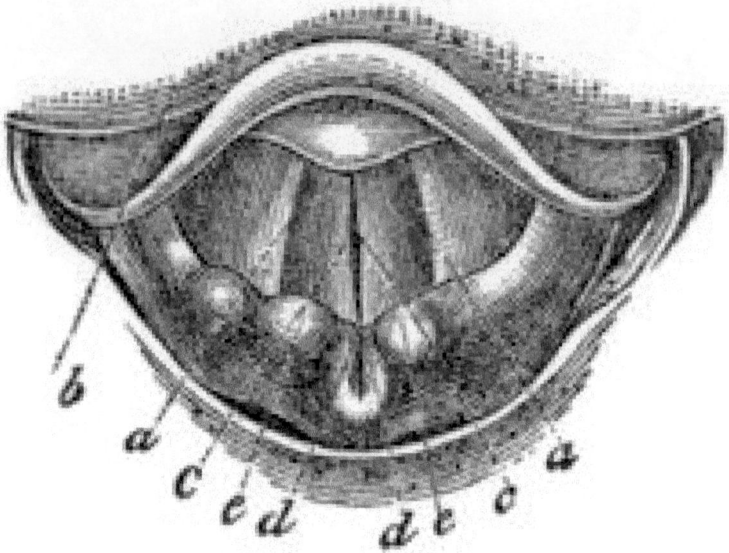

Representation in the mirror of the vocal organ in giving out sound.

a. Superior or false vocal ligaments, or chords.

b. Epiglottis.

c. Inferior or true vocal ligaments.

d. Arytenoid cartilages.

e. Capitula Santorini.

When, in using the laryngoscope upon myself, I slowly sang the ascending scale, this movement of the vocal chords and arytenoid cartilages was repeated at every tone. They separated and appeared to retreat, in order to close again anew, and to rise somewhat more than before. This movement of the arytenoid cartilages may best be compared to that of a pair of scissors. With every higher tone the vocal ligaments seemed more stretched and the glottis somewhat shorter.—[The glottis is a term applied to the space occupied by the vocal chords (the lips of the glottis): when separated, we say the glottis is open, when they touch, that it is closed.]—At the same time, when I sang the scale upward, beginning with the lowest tones, the vocal ligaments seemed to be moved in their whole length and breadth by large, loose vibrations, which extended even to all the rest of the interior of the larynx.

The place at which the arytenoid cartilages, almost closed together, cease their action and leave the formation of the sound to the vocal ligaments alone, I found in the entire vibration of the glottis, or in the chest register of the female voice, at do do♯ [musical notation], more rarely at si [musical notation]. In the chest register of the male voice this change occurs at la si♭ [musical notation]. With some effort the above-mentioned action of the arytenoid cartilages may be continued several tones higher. But such tones, especially in the female voice, have that rough and common timbre which we are too often compelled to hear in our female singers. The glottis also, in this case, as well as the parts of the larynx near the glottis, betrays the effort very plainly; as the tones ascend, they grow more and more red. *Thus, as at this place in the chest register there occurs a visible and sensible straining of the organs, so also is it in all the remaining transitions, as soon as the attempt is made to extend the action by which the lower tones are formed beyond the given limits of the same.* These transitions, which cannot be extended without effort, coincide perfectly with the places where *J. Müller* had to *stretch* the ligaments of his exsected larynx so powerfully in order to reach the succeeding half-tone. Garcia likewise finds tones thus formed disagreeable and imperfect in sound (*klanglos*).

Usually, therefore, at the note do♯ [musical notation] in the female voice, and la si♭ [musical notation] in the male voice, the vocal ligaments alone act in forming the sound, and throughout the register are moved by large, loose, full vibrations (*Totalschwingungen*). But the instant the vocal ligaments are deprived of the assistance of the arytenoid cartilages, they relax and appear longer than at the last tone produced by that aid. But with every higher tone they appear again to be stretched shorter and more powerfully up to fa fa♯ [musical notation], the natural transition of both the chest and falsetto registers, as well in the *male* as in the *female*. The larynx is perceptibly lower in all the tones of the chest register than in quiet breathing.

THE FALSETTO REGISTER

All the tones of the falsetto register are produced by vibrations only of the fine, inner, slender edges of the vocal ligaments. In this action the vocal ligaments are not so near together, but allow of a fine linear space between them, and the superior ligaments are pressed farther back than in the production of the tones of the chest register. The rest of the action of the glottis is, however, entirely the same. With the beginning of the falsetto register at fa♯ , the whole glottis appears again longer, and the vocal ligaments are much looser than in the highest tones of the chest register. The united action, already described, of the arytenoid cartilages and the ligaments in forming the deeper tones of the chest register, extends to do

do♯ in the female voice, and in the male voice to mi♭ mi

commonly written thus: mi♭ mi but which only rarely occurs in composition, and then is sung by tenorists as I have given it; that is, one octave lower.

With the do♯ in the female voice and the mi♭ mi

in the male voice, the arytenoid cartilages cease again to act, and as before, at the second higher series of tones of the chest register, leave the formation of the sounds to the vocal ligaments alone, which at this change appear again longer and looser, but with every higher tone tighten up

to fa fa♯ in the female voice, and in the male voice to sol

, or as it is commonly written: . In the falsetto register the larynx preserves its natural position, as in quiet breathing.

THE HEAD REGISTER

When in the observation of the falsetto register I had sung upwards to its highest tones, and then sang still higher, I became aware with the fa

of a change in the motions of the organ of singing, and the tones thus produced had a different timbre from the falsetto tones. It required long and patient practice before I finally succeeded in drawing back the epiglottis so that I could see the glottis in its whole length. Not until then was I able to observe the following:

With the fa , the vocal ligaments suddenly closed firmly together to their middle, with their fine edges one over the other.

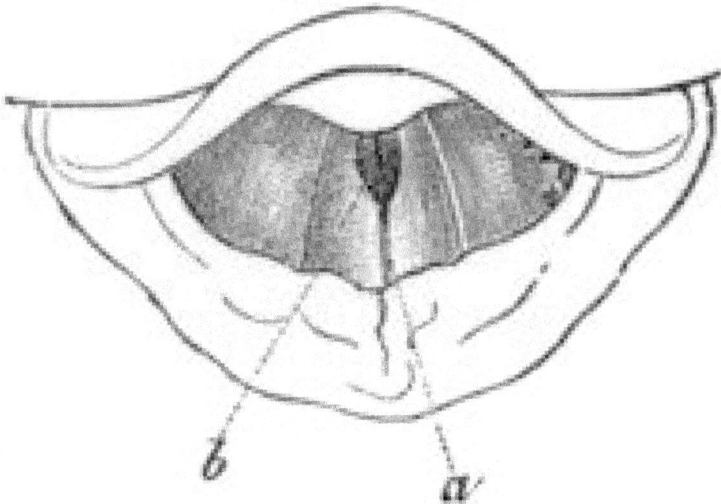

Representation in the mirror of the organ of singing in the formation of head tones.

a. The closing together of the vocal ligaments.

b. Open part of the glottis.

The oval opening of the anterior portion of the glottis is imperfectly shown, because it is hidden from view by the epiglottis at the extreme end.

This closing appeared as a fine red line extending from the arytenoid cartilages at the back forward to the middle of the vocal ligaments, and leaving free only a third part of the whole glottis, immediately under the epiglottis, to the front wall of the larynx.

The foremost part of the glottis formed an oval orifice, which, with each higher tone, seemed to contract more and more, and so became smaller and rounder. The fine edges of the vocal ligaments which formed this orifice were alone vibrating, and the vibrations seemed at first looser, but, with every higher tone, the ligaments were more stretched. The larynx remained in its natural state.

Only after I had frequently repeated this observation of the head tones in myself and in others, and had always arrived at the same results, did I venture to publish it. The most various conjectures respecting the formation of the head voice had been previously proposed by the learned, and the existence, even, of the head voice had been denied by *Bataille.* It would lead us too far away to make mention here of all these different views, which, with the exception of those of *Dr. Merkel of Leipzig,* showed themselves to be really without a sound foundation.

It was objected to the results of my observations, that such an action of the glottis "was only possible by means of cartilages and muscles, but that such cartilages and muscles as could render an action of that kind possible were not known, nor was there any reference to them to be found in any manual of anatomy." While I fully admitted the soundness of this objection, I was, after repeated observations, more and more convinced of the correctness of my own statements. But as I found nothing to support them in any anatomical work, either German or French, I began anew to study the anatomy of the larynx in dissected subjects.

My renewed efforts were rewarded by the discovery, within the membranes of the vocal ligaments, of those filaments or fibres of muscle which in the anatomical Appendix to this book I mention as *arytenoid-thyroid interna,* and which have also been found by other observers. They are found in all larynxes, and consist of muscular fibres, sometimes finer, sometimes thicker.[3]

At the same time I satisfied myself of the existence of a pair of cartilages— the cuneiform cartilages described in the Appendix. I found these always in the female larynx, but only now and then in the male. As these cartilages, also found within the membranes of the vocal ligaments and reaching from their junction with the arytenoid cartilages to the middle of the ligaments, are only now and then fully formed in the male larynx, but undeniably work the shutting part of the glottis, it follows plainly that only a few male voices are capable of producing the head tones.

But observation with the microscope revealed in those larynxes in which the cuneiform cartilages were wanting, parts of a cartilaginous mass, or the rudiments of a cartilage, in the place indicated.

For anatomical investigations the male larynx is commonly used, its muscles being more powerful and its cartilages firmer than in the female larynx, and this explains why anatomists in Germany have been reluctant to admit the existence of the cuneiform cartilages. It was, therefore, a great satisfaction to me to find them described under the name of cuneiform cartilages in *Wilson's Human Anatomy*, with the remark that they are sometimes wanting.[4]

The head register possesses a very great capacity of expansion, which, without the slightest straining, may be gradually extended, with some practice, a whole octave, and often even still farther upwards. When the transition is made from the highest tones of the falsetto register to the head register, there is experienced the same sense of relief in the organs of singing as in passing from the chest to the falsetto register. And this is very easy to be understood, because the ligaments by this repeated partial closure of the glottis are much less stretched than in the highest tones of the preceding lower register. The difference in sound between the highest tones of the falsetto and head registers is often slight, on which account these two registers, so different in their mechanism, are easily confounded. Only in entirely healthy vocal organs can the head tones be observed. A too great secretion of mucus, or any inflammation of the mucous membrane, embarrasses the formation of head and falsetto tones, while the vibrations of the fine edges of the vocal ligaments are thereby obstructed. The character of the vocal organ fully explains why in the case of sick or of worn-out voices it is always the high tones that are first lost. When I have observed, in the sick, irritation of the mucous membrane, I have often found the oval orifice which is formed in the production of the head tones entirely covered with mucus. In my own case, when by repeated effort this bubble of mucus broke,

instead of the a^2 , which I meant to be sounded, there came the a^3, an octave higher, which in perfect health it was never possible for me to reach. I have observed the same phenomenon sometimes in my pupils.

When one sings the scale, note by note downwards, one can sing with the action of the higher register many of the tones of the lower, without any observable straining of the organ; indeed, there is a perceptible feeling of relief; only these tones are not so full as when sung in their natural register.

ABNORMAL MOVEMENTS OF THE GLOTTIS

Garcia states, in his observations, that sometimes when the rims of the vocal ligaments have come together, there remains between the arytenoid cartilages a triangular space, which does not close until the tone is produced. *Czermak* likewise describes this process in his pathological investigations, and also a similar one with the laryngoscope. While, namely, the arytenoid cartilages seem to be wholly closed, one sees just before the beginning of the tone the vocal ligaments standing apart in a square-shaped form, and only closing together with the tone. At first, before I had attained to much practice in observation, I often saw these processes in myself, and later often in others.

That these accidental forms of the glottis bear no relation to the generation of sounds, as *Funke* truly says, is made evident by an irregularity in the combined action of the muscles of the larynx, by which the coming together of the arytenoid cartilages takes place later than that of the ligaments, or that of the ligaments later than that of the arytenoid cartilages.

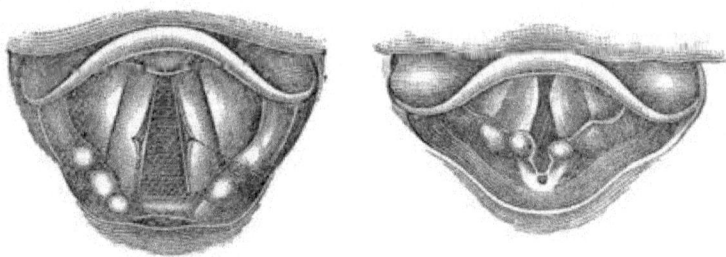

As recently great importance has often been ascribed to these abnormal movements of the glottis in the generation of sound, I have felt bound to mention them.

RESULTS OF THE FOREGOING OBSERVATIONS

In consequence of the observations above described, the following facts may be established:

I. We have found five different actions of the vocal organ:

1. *The first series of tones of the chest register*, in which the whole glottis is moved by large, loose vibrations, and the arytenoid cartilages with the vocal ligaments are in action.

2. *The second series of the chest register*, when the vocal ligaments alone act, and are likewise moved by large, loose vibrations.

3. *The first series of the falsetto register*, where again the whole glottis, consisting of the arytenoid cartilages and vocal ligaments, is in action, the very fine interior edges of the ligaments, however, being alone in vibrating motion.

4. *The second series of the falsetto register*, the tones of which are generated by the vibrations of the edges alone of the vocal ligaments.

5. *The head register*, in the same manner and by the same vibrations, and with a partial closing of the vocal ligaments.

II. We have learned the transitions of the registers, i. e., those tones where a different action of the vocal organ takes place; and observation has further taught us that these *natural limits of the registers cannot be exceeded without a straining that may be both seen and felt*; that is, that we may not preserve the action of a lower series for the tones of a higher. On the other hand, the vocal organs show *no straining* when the action of a higher series of tones is kept for a lower, only the fulness of the tones is thereby diminished.

III. We have further seen that *only the transition from the chest register to the falsetto*

is in all voices at the same tones, the fa fa ; but, both in men's and women's voices, the other *transitions of the registers are different*. As the male larynx is about a third larger than the female, it is plain that the registers in the male voice have a greater expansion. The transitions, however, in the tenor, as in the bass, are at the same tones, and only sometimes a half tone higher or lower in one voice than in another. The organs of the man are stronger and harder than those of the woman, and they are not often capable of producing tones with the vibrations of the edges of the vocal ligaments (falsetto tones), but the lower series of tones of the chest register has, in such voices, a much greater extension downwards. *The difference between the bass and tenor voices lies in the greater or less ease with which the tones of the higher or lower registers are sung, and in the greater fulness and beauty, always connected therewith, of the higher or lower register, that is, in the timbre of the voice*; not, as is commonly thought, in the difference of the transitions of the registers.

The same is also the case with the female voice; *as well in the contralto as in the soprano voice the transitions of the registers are at the same tones*, and the difference of the voices lies only in the timbre, and in the greater facility with which the higher or lower tones are produced, and not in the different compass of the voice.

The transitions of the registers are:

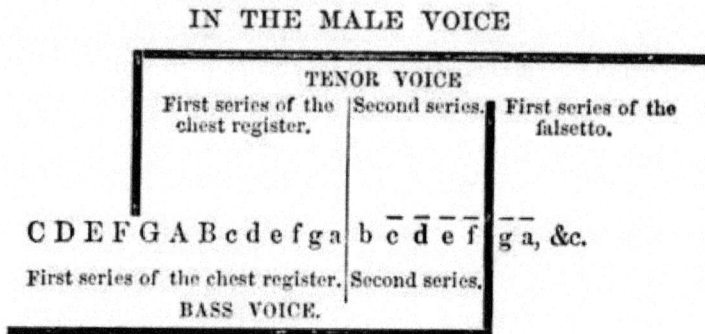

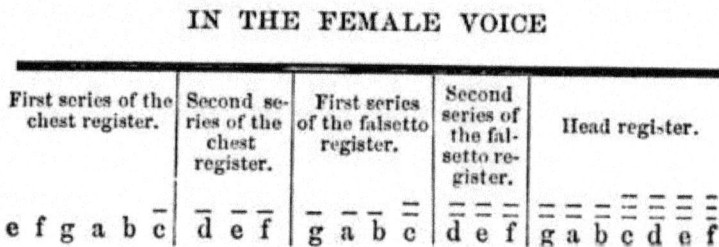

IN THE MALE VOICE

TENOR VOICE		
First series of the chest register.	Second series.	First series of the falsetto.

C D E F G A B c d e f g a | b c̄ d̄ ē f̄ | g a, &c.

First series of the chest register.	Second series.
BASS VOICE.	

IN THE FEMALE VOICE

First series of the chest register.	Second series of the chest register.	First series of the falsetto register.	Second series of the falsetto register.	Head register.
e f g a b c̄	d̄ e f	g a b c̄	d̄ e f	g a b c d e f

The investigation and discovery of the facts here stated have been made with the utmost conscientiousness, repeated by men of science in Germany, and acknowledged as correct.

PRACTICAL APPLICATION OF THESE OBSERVATIONS TO THE CULTIVATION OF THE SINGING VOICE

In teaching the art of singing, it is now-a-days very generally the custom to endeavor to raise the lower registers as far as possible toward the higher. This is especially the case with the tenor voice. It is considered a special advantage in a tenor voice when it can sing the a[1] on the first leger line

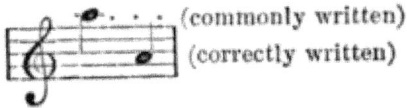

(commonly written)
(correctly written)

with the chest register.

Upwards of a hundred and fifty years ago, when every good tenor was required to sing a¹ with a clear, full chest tone, this note, according to the orchestra pitch then, was not higher than a note between f and f♯, according to the present orchestra pitch in England and America. Since that time the orchestra pitch has everywhere gradually risen so imperceptibly that this important fact remained unknown to many singers and teachers, and until recently has been only rarely noticed. And yet it is precisely this much higher pitch and the consequent unnatural extension of the limits of the registers, which is the chief cause why most voices now-a-days last so little while.

That the registers may be forced up beyond their limits is possible, we have seen. But observation teaches us that it cannot be done without a straining of the organs which may be both seen and felt, and no organ will bear continued over-straining. It will gradually be weakened thereby, and become at last wholly useless.

This is a simple fact, scientifically established, universally known. It admits, therefore, of no doubt that the common custom of forcing the registers beyond their natural bounds injures voices, and seriously affects their durability. Even when the organs are so strong that they can bear the unnatural effort for a considerable length of time, they gain nothing in grace and timbre. Like every thing else unnatural, it carries with it its own punishment. Our tenor singers are, for the most part, only for a few years in full possession of their voices, while the earlier singers knew how to keep their voices fine and full to their latest age.

Not until 1858, when the orchestra pitch in Paris had risen for a¹ to 448 vibrations in a second, and tenors were no longer able to reach it with the chest register, was general attention turned to this evil. The Academy at that time fixed the orchestra pitch at 435 vibrations a second for a¹. This pitch is now introduced almost universally in Germany, and it is a full half note lower than our usual orchestra pitch in America. The introduction of the Paris pitch is, however, of no great advantage so long as singers and teachers keep to the same limits of the registers that they had at the beginning of the seventeenth century, when a¹ had 404 vibrations in a second, and was about a third lower than our present a¹. Musicians are averse to the introduction of this old low pitch, as the instruments are no longer accommodated to it. And besides, it is not at all necessary, if only singers and teachers would observe it better, and either set their pieces a third lower, or sing the notes that are difficult to be reached with a lower register in a natural way and with a higher register.

The old Italian masters were proud of being able so to educate the falsetto register of a tenor voice that it was difficult to distinguish chest tones and falsetto tones from one another, even for an ear accustomed to observe the finest distinctions of sound. And this art is by no means so difficult as is supposed, and is not dependent on the natural strength of the first falsetto tones. When in the male organ there exists the power of bringing the edges of the vocal ligaments into vibratory motion, and when these tones at the beginning, compared with the chest tones of the same voice, are weak and thin, then they may, with skill and perseverance, be trained to quite similar fulness.

That the male voice requires far more time and practice than the female to effect an imperceptible transition from the chest register to the falsetto, is unquestionable. And while this transition is always so very apparent in the man's voice, it is often scarcely observable to a practiced ear even in uncultivated female voices. Women, in speaking, always use the second chest and the first falsetto register, continually passing from one to the other of these registers without any change in the position of the mouth or of the resonance apparatus of the voice. They are thus all their lives long unconsciously practicing this transition, and because of this equal physical use of the chest and falsetto notes, the great physiological difference of these two registers almost entirely disappears. Although men do not use the falsetto register in speaking, it is not yet proved to be impossible for the male voice to attain the same results as the female.

When in the beginning the falsetto tones are sung always *piano* and very *staccato*, by long-continued, careful practice, with entirely the same physical treatment of both registers, a smooth and natural transition from one to the other is most easily obtained. Thus the falsetto tones gain more and more in fulness and strength, and sound far more agreeably than the forced-up chest tones of our tenorists, sung with swollen-out throats and blood-red faces.

The education of men's voices involves many difficulties which do not exist in the case of the voices of women. Almost all men speak and sing in one register—tenors mostly in the second chest register, bassos mostly in the first, and oftentimes indeed not even in a correct natural manner. With this one register they sing as high and as low as they can, and this they consider the whole compass of their voices. The low chest register is rarely found good and natural (as regards the beauty of sound). In order for the production of these low chest tones, to set the vocal chords vibrating in their whole length and breadth, it is necessary that a fuller column of air from the lungs should press upon the glottis through the windpipe, which is readily of itself enlarged thereby. The easier and the more naturally this takes place, the more beautifully and naturally do these tones sound. Under the delusion that only strong singing is beautiful, and that this can be achieved only by extraordinary exertion, most of our basso singers have a peculiar way of pressing out the windpipe, which is not only very fatiguing, but gives to the low tones a rough, disagreeable sound. Among public speakers also this exhausting, faulty way of bringing out the chest tones is not uncommon, frequently rendering their voices quite incapable of use. *Merkel* represents this way of forming the low tones as a peculiar register, which he calls the *Strohbassregister*, and through him a quite prevalent bad habit has found in other scientific works a right to existence which by no means belongs to it.

The female voice is treated in the same unnatural way. Many teachers teach their pupils to sing with the lower series of the chest register as high up as

possible, often to the e¹ f¹   , as far as the organs permit, and then let them begin the falsetto register. In this way the second series of the chest register is entirely omitted; but the made tones, as the expression is, thus obtained, sound very disagreeable and coarse, and the falsetto tones, which in this way begin lower than necessary, are on the contrary faint and weak. Of the falsetto register these teachers commonly require only the first

series, up to d² e♭²   , to be sung, and then directly begin the head tones. Thus the second series of the falsetto is not used; but the tones belonging to it, which are sung with the first series of the falsetto register, are for the most part hard and sharp and seldom pure, while the tones of the head voice, coming in too soon, are thin and unmusical, and the whole voice thus receives an irregular formation. Many teachers, again, allow the lower tones of the chest register to be sung with the higher series of the same, whereby these tones are naturally never as sweet and strong. Then, too, they

press the first series of the falsetto up to d² e♭²   , and thence, as far as it is possible, the voice is to ascend with the second series of the falsetto, without admitting the head tones, even in voices with the high soprano timbre. But the tones thus forced up are for the most part sharp and destitute of all grace. And it is just this that is one of the commonest faults of our present mode of singing.

As it has been customary to cultivate, in the male voice only, the three lower series, because both of the highest sound sweet and graceful only from the soft, delicate organs of the female voice, and as the male voice is rarely capable of compassing the highest series, the erroneous idea has gradually obtained prevalence among teachers of singing, that there are only three different series of tones, and that the female voice has only two transitions.

In voices fresh and unvitiated the different series are very easily distinguished by their different timbre. One hears this difference of timbre most clearly in the transition of the second series of the chest register into the falsetto in the male voice, and in the female voice at the transition of the first series of the falsetto register into the second.

As has been observed, the larynx stands lower with the tones of the chest register than with the tones of the other registers, or during quiet breathing.

In order, in the low chest tones, to bring the whole glottis into full vibration, the air, as it is expired, must press upon it with a larger volume. From all parts of the lungs the air, when expired, presses into the windpipe, the rings of which, widening as much as possible, come somewhat nearer to each other and draw down the larynx.

One has thus the sensation as if the whole body took part in this formation of sound, and as if the lower tones of the chest register were drawn from the lowest part of the lungs.

In producing the second series of the chest register, the sensation is as if the tones came from the upper part of the chest, midway between the pit of the stomach and the larynx.

With regard to the tones of the first series of the falsetto, the feeling is as if they had their origin in the throat.

In the tones of the second series of the falsetto, we feel as if the throat had nothing to do with them—as if they were formed above, in the mouth.

With the head tones, one has the feeling that they come from the forehead.

It is these *physical sensations* that have given occasion to many erroneous conjectures in regard to the formation of tones, but we are satisfied that they have no direct relation to the generation of sound, and appear so only through the nerves active in the process.

By directing the attention of one's pupils to these different sensations, it is very easy to make them acquainted with the different registers of the voice—always a very necessary proceeding in the first training of a voice, although it seems to be so only in the case of such voices as have been previously misdirected.

The culture of the female voice is best begun with the two series of the falsetto register and the second of the chest register; the tones of these three middle registers must be pretty well cultivated before the lowest chest tones and the head voice are begun to be formed. The voice in this way best attains to an equal fulness. It is self-evident also that the teaching should be such that the transitions of the registers should be not at all or scarcely perceptible, consequently that all the tones should sound proportionally strong and full.

In the soprano voice the falsetto, and in the contralto voice the chest register, have more fulness and grace, and thus we may distinguish to which kind of voice a voice belongs, for the compass of the voice is not always confined within certain limits. There are contraltos that can sing the high head tones with ease, and sopranos that can sing the low chest tones with equal facility— a fact which has often given occasion to an incorrect treatment of a voice. So also with the male voice. A bass voice sings the lower series of the chest register with more ease and sweetness and with more obscure timbre. A tenor voice sings the second series of the chest register in a clearer timbre.

The baritone and mezzo-soprano voices, so called—that is, such voices as have a limited compass, and cannot sing either the highest or the lowest tones—are by no means so numerous as they are thought to be. The best tenor voices, which cannot naturally reach the lowest bass tones, and whose organs do not allow of an unnatural forcing up beyond the higher limits of the chest register, are commonly pronounced baritone voices, for no one now-a-days thinks of cultivating the falsetto register of the male voice.

Few teachers, likewise, understand how to teach correctly the tones of the head register. If a soprano voice cannot readily and agreeably sing the low contralto tones, and extend the falsetto scale far enough upwards beyond its limit, it is reckoned among the mezzo-soprano voices. The celebrated singing master *Thomaselli*, of *Padua*, maintained that baritone and mezzo-soprano voices "had no existence in nature, but were only the products of our false methods of instruction."

I have sometimes found mezzo-soprano and baritone voices, but not in so great number by far as the four chief kinds of voices—bass, tenor, contralto, and soprano.

Although an exact knowledge of the vocal organ and its various actions must be required of a teacher before the education of a voice can be committed to him, yet it would be unwise to undertake to teach singing by means of scientific explanations without sufficient previous knowledge; the pupil would, in this case, understand as little of what he was about and be as little helped as a child learning to read would be assisted by one who merely sought to make intelligible to him the mechanism by which sound is formed. The most natural and the simplest way in singing, as in all things else, is the best. Let the teacher sing correctly every tone to his pupil until the latter knows how to imitate it, and his ear has learned how to distinguish the different timbres.[5]

The discovery of the natural transitions of the registers has brought to light one of the greatest evils of our present mode of singing, and shown at the same time how wanting in durability are the voices of those of our artists whose aim and endeavor it is to force the registers upward beyond their natural limits. Although the concert pitch is so very much higher now than it was in the most flourishing period of the singing art, yet no regard is paid to this fact in the education of a voice, and our tenorists try to reach the a¹

with the chest register, just as they did one hundred and fifty years ago.

In the ignorance existing concerning the natural transitions of the registers, and in the unnatural forcing of the voice, is found a chief cause of the decline of the art of singing. And the present inability to preserve the voice is the consequence of a method of teaching unnatural, and therefore imposing too great a strain upon the voice. [6]

No one who has not made the art of singing a special study, can form any idea of the obscure and conflicting views in regard to the transitions of the registers which prevail among singing teachers and artists. Almost every teacher has a peculiar theory of his own in regard to the formation of the voice; every one has his own views, sometimes extremely fanciful, of the formation of tones and of the registers—views to which he tenaciously adheres, summarily rejecting all others. Almost as at the building of the tower of Babel, one teacher scarcely understands any longer what another means, and instead of harmonious endeavors to improve the art, teachers of singing are commonly found disputing among themselves.

To bring light and order into such a chaos can only be accomplished by the most thorough scientific study, and even then it is an undertaking of the greatest difficulty. Custom stands in the way as an antagonist, and there must be a conflict with long-cherished and wide-spread errors and prejudices. It lies also in the nature of the case that teachers of singing are the most determined opponents to be encountered. It is very hard for this class, and it demands of them no common self-denial to acknowledge and renounce as errors what they have taught for years and held to be truths. Those teachers, however, who have made the necessary sacrifice, have been compensated with the richest success; and such, we trust, will in all cases be the result, and so the path be broken for the true and the natural.

It will be perhaps comparatively easy to advance the art of singing in America; for, as Humboldt says, not entirely without truth, the Germans require for every improvement two centuries—one to find out the need of it, and another to make it.

2 It must be remarked that the diagrams here given are copies of *reflected* images, and therefore the upper side of the representation shows the front of the larynx, and the lower the farther side of the larynx.

3 In recent works on laryngoscopy they are often described as continuations or parts of one of the principal muscles of the larynx.

4 In recent French and English works upon laryngoscopy, the cuneiform cartilages are frequently mentioned, and sometimes confounded with the cartilages Wrisbergi.

5 On this account the male voice should be trained by men and the female voice by women. For, as it is impossible for a man to give to a female pupil a correct perception of the tones of the head register and of the second series of the falsetto, with its peculiar female timbre, so is it impossible for a woman to sing and teach correctly the deep, sonorous chest tones of the male voice. *Frederick Wiek*, that admirable teacher, who perceives intuitively what is natural and true in instruction, has an excellent expedient. In his hours of instruction he avails himself of the aid of young women with practised voices, who sing every exercise to his female pupils until the latter are able to imitate them correctly.

6 Voices which by this overstrained and unnatural way of singing have become worn-out and useless may by correct, proper treatment recover, even at an advanced age, their former grace and power; and even those chronic inflammations of the larynx which are so difficult of treatment may be cured by a natural and moderate exercise of the voice in singing.

III
PHYSICAL VIEW
FORMATION OF SOUNDS BY THE VOCAL ORGAN

FOR the artistic culture of the singing voice the knowledge of the physiological processes during the formation of tones does not suffice. This knowledge brings us acquainted only with the instrument, the artistic treatment of which is to be learned. Having, therefore, in the preceding pages stated the most important points in the formation of tones, physiologically considered, we are now to consider more nearly the physical laws relating to the same, especially as the physical view of the subject, through the latest investigations and discoveries of Prof. Helmholtz, in Heidelberg, has so much importance for music in general. In order, however, to present a clear view of this branch of our subject, in so far as the recent advances of science can be practically applied to the improvement of the art of singing, we must recur to those natural laws which are doubtless well known to most of our readers.

In order to bring the external world to our consciousness, we are provided with various organs of sense; and as the eye is sensible to the light, the ear is sensible to sound, which comes to our consciousness either as noise (*Geräusch*) or as tone (*Klang*). The whistling of the wind, the plashing of water, the rattling of a wagon are noises, but musical instruments give us tones. When, however, many untuned instruments sound together, or when all the keys within an octave are struck on the same time, then it is a noise that we hear. Tones are therefore more simple and regular than noises. The ear perceives both by means of the agitation of the air that surrounds us. In the case of noise the agitation of the air is an irregularly changing motion. In musical sounds, on the other hand, there is a movement of the air in a continuously regular manner, which must be caused by a similar movement in the body which gives the sound. These so-called periodical movements of the sound in the body, rising, falling and repeated at equal intervals, are called vibrations. The length of the interval elapsing between one movement and the next succeeding repetition of the same movement is called the duration of vibration (*Schwingungsdauer*), or period of motion.

TONE, AND ITS LAWS OF VIBRATION

A *tone* is produced by a periodical motion of the sounding body—a *noise* by motions *not* periodical. We can see and feel the sounding vibrations of stationary bodies. The eye can perceive the vibrations of a string, and a person playing on a clarionet, oboe, or any similar instrument, feels the vibration of the reed of the mouthpiece. How the movements of the air, agitated by the vibrations of the stationary body, are felt by the ear as tone (*Klang*), Helmholtz illustrates by the motion of waves of water in the following way: Imagine a stone thrown into perfectly smooth water. Around the point of the surface struck by the stone there is instantly formed a little ring, which, moving outwards equally in all directions, spreads to an ever-enlarging circle. Corresponding to this ring, sound goes out in the air from an agitated point, and enlarges in all directions as far as the limits of the atmosphere permit. What goes on in the air is essentially the same that takes place on the surface of the water; the chief difference only is that sound spreads out in the spacious sea of air like a sphere, while the waves on the surface of the water can extend only like a circle. At the surface the mass of the water is free to rise upward, where it is compressed and forms billows, or crests. In the interior of the aerial ocean the air must be condensed, because it cannot rise. For, "in fact, the condensation of the sound-wave corresponds to the crest, while the rarefaction of the sound-wave corresponds to the sinus of the water-wave."[1]

The water-waves press continually onwards into the distance, but the particles of the water move to and fro periodically within narrow limits. One may easily see these two movements by observing a small piece of wood floating on water; the wood moves just as the particles of water in contact with it move. It is not carried along with the rings of the wave, but is tossed up and down, and at last remains in the same place where it was at the first. In a similar way, as the particles of water around the wood are moved by the ring only in passing, so the waves of sound spread onwards through new strata of air, while the particles of air, tossed to and fro by these waves as they pass, are never really moved by them from their first place. A drop falling upon the surface of the water creates in it only a single agitation; but when a regular series of drops falls upon it, every drop produces a ring on the water. Every ring passes over the surface just like its predecessor, and is followed by other rings in the same way. In this way there is produced on the water a regular series of rings ever expanding. As many drops as fall into the water in a second, so many waves will in a second strike a floating piece of wood, which will be just so many times tossed up and down, and thus have a periodical motion, the period of which corresponds with the interval at which the drops fall. In like manner a sounding body, periodically moved, produces a similar periodic movement, first of the air, and then of the drum in the ear; the duration of the vibrations constituting the movement must be the same in the ear as in the sounding body.

THE PROPERTIES OF TONE (KLANG)

The sounds produced by such periodic agitations of the air have three peculiar properties: 1. STRENGTH, 2. PITCH, 3. TIMBRE.

The strength of the tone depends on the greater or less breadth of its vibrations, that is, of the waves of sound, the higher or lower pitch of the tones upon the number of the vibrations; that is, the tones are always higher the greater the number of the vibrations, or lower the less the number of the vibrations. A second is used as the unit of time, and by number of vibrations is understood the number of vibrations which the sounding body gives forth in a second of time. The tones used in music lie between 40 and 4000 vibrations per second, in the extent of seven octaves. The tones which we can perceive lie between 16 and 38,000 vibrations to the second, within the compass of eleven octaves. The later pianos usually go as low as C_1 with 33, or even to A_2 with $27\frac{1}{2}$ vibrations; mostly as high as a^4 or c^5, with 3520 and 4224 vibrations. The one lined a^1, from which all instruments are tuned, has now usually 440 to 450 vibrations to the second in England and America. The French Academy, however, has recently established for the same note 435 vibrations, and this lower tuning has already been universally introduced in Germany.[8]

The high octave of a tone has in the same time exactly double the number of vibrations of the tone itself. Suppose, therefore, that a tone has 50 vibrations in a second, its octave has 100 in the same time; i. e., twice as many. The octave above this has 200 vibrations, &c. The Pythagoreans knew this acoustic law of the ascending tones, and that the octave of a tone had twice as many vibrations in a second as the tone itself, and that the fifth above the first octave had three times as many; the second octave, four times; the major third above the second octave, five times as many; the fifth of the same octave, six times; the small seventh of the same octave, seven times. In notation it would be thus, if we take as the lowest note C, for example:

The figures below the lines denote how many times greater the number of vibrations is than that of the first tone. In the first octave we find only one tone; in the second, two; in the third, all the tones of the major chord with the minor seventh. In the fourth octave we find sixteen tones (which, however, we divide in our system of music into twelve). Likewise, we find in the fifth octave thirty-two tones, which number is doubled in the sixth. Hence, the Greeks had quarter and eighth tones, which we in our equal-tempered tuning have done away with.[9]

The production of a higher pitch in a tone rests in all sounding bodies upon the uniform law which we may observe in the strings of musical instruments, whose tones ascend either by greater tension, by shortening, or through a diminution of the density of the strings.

THE TIMBRE (KLANGFARBE) OF TONES

Strength and pitch were the first two distinctions of different tones. The third is the timbre. When we hear one and the same tone sounded successively upon a violin, trumpet, clarionet, oboe, upon a piano, or by a human voice, &c., although it is of the same strength and of the same pitch, yet the tone of all these instruments is different, and we very easily distinguish the instrument from which it comes. The changes of the timbre seem to be infinitely manifold; for, not to mention the fact that we have a multitude of different musical instruments, all which can give the same tone, letting alone also that different instruments of the same kind as well as different voices show certain differences of timbre, the very same tone can be given upon one and the same instrument, or by one and the same voice, with manifold differences of timbre.[10]

As now the strength of the tone is determined by the breadth of the vibrations, and the pitch by their number, so the varieties of timbre are ascribed to the different forms of the waves of vibration. For as the surface of the water is stirred differently by the falling into it of a stone, by the blowing over it of the wind, or the passing through it of a ship, &c., so the movements of the air take different shapes from sounding bodies. The movement proceeding from the string of a violin over which the bow is drawn, is different from those movements caused by the hammer of a piano or by a clarionet.

OVER-TONES (OBERTÖNE)

That timbre is dependent on the form of the vibrations is confirmed by Helmholtz, and acknowledged as so far correct that every different timbre requires a different vibratory form, but different forms sometimes correspond to nearly the same timbre. But how far the different forms of vibration correspond with different timbres, Helmholtz shows by a fact which has hitherto escaped the notice of physicists, although it forms the foundation of all music. We have learned by the stereoscope that we have two different views of every object, and compose a third view from those two. *Just so the ear perceives different musical tones which come to our consciousness only as one tone.*

It is in general, and especially in the case of the human voice, very difficult to distinguish these single parts of tone, because we are accustomed to take the impressions of the external world without analyzing them, and only with a view to their use.

But when we are once convinced of the existence of partial tones (*Partialtöne*), if we concentrate our attention, we can also distinguish them. The ear hears, then, not only that tone, the pitch of which is determined, as we have shown, by the duration of its vibrations, but a whole series of tones besides, which Helmholtz names "*the harmonic over-tones*" of the tone, in opposition to that first tone (fundamental tone) which is the lowest among them all, generally the strongest also, and according to the pitch of which we decide the pitch of the tone. The series of these over-tones is for each musical tone precisely the same; they are, namely, the tones of the so-called acoustic series, arising, as already described, from the doubling of the vibrations. First, the fundamental tone, then its octave with twice as many vibrations, then the fifth of this octave, &c.

The different timbre of tones thus depends upon the different forms of the vibrations, whence arise various relations of the fundamental tone to the over-tones as they vary in strength. The most thorough inquiries have led to the following results, of the first importance in every formation of tone: *that the appropriate form of the vibratory waves which is the most agreeable to the ear, as well as the fullest, softest and most beautiful timbre which corresponds to that form, is produced when the fundamental tone, and the over-tones following it, so sound that the fundamental tone and the over-tones sound together, the former most strongly, while the latter are heard fainter and fainter in the intervals of the major chord with the minor seventh, so that, with the fundamental tone, still further sound seven over-tones.* If the higher harmonic over-tones grow stronger, and even overpower the fundamental tone, the sound grows shriller, but when the discordant over-tones lying close together, higher than the tones just named, overpower the fundamental tone, the timbre becomes sharp and disagreeable.

But these over-tones are not to be confounded with the earlier known combination-tones (*Combinationstöne*), which arise from the sounding together of two consonant intervals, and likewise have their own over-tones.

Prof. Helmholtz has by means of his Resonance and Electrical apparatus invented aids by which the forms of the vibrations can be perceived as well as the over-tones, and the different degrees of strength of the latter in relation to one another and to the fundamental tone can be exactly measured. In attempting by means of the above-mentioned apparatus to cause the several over-tones to sound more or less strongly with the fundamental tone, and again entirely to veil others, it became possible to Prof. Helmholtz to produce artificially most opposite timbres, as well as all the vowels of speech.

Even when, in the culture of a voice, we have advanced so far that none of the inharmonic but only the harmonic over-tones sound with the fundamental tone, we shall always find that every voice has its own peculiar *Klangfarbe*—i. e., its own characteristic timbre; and it is not possible so to form the tones of a voice that the over-tones sounding with them shall diminish proportionally according to their height. Every voice has one, mostly two, over-tones, which always predominate in every tone, every register, and give the voice its peculiar quality. When, with the first octave, the fifth above it sounds, the voice is full and mellow. A clear, sympathetic, silvery ring is produced by the sounding of the seventh with the octave immediately above it. One of the most beautiful timbres is a result of the prominence of the third with the seventh, etc. This peculiarity appears to be connected with the particular form and structure of the cavity of the mouth. That parts of the cavity of the mouth serve as a sounding-board in the formation of sound, has already been mentioned.[11]

The perfection of a tone at a certain pitch depends, in the resonance of the cavity of the mouth, upon the utterance of some vowel, to which the parts of the mouth are adjusted; and this perfection is considerably affected by even a slight variation in the timbre of the vowel, as it occurs in different dialects of the same language. On the other hand, the peculiar tones of the cavity of the mouth are almost wholly independent of age and sex. The peculiar pitch of the resonance apparatus has also an influence upon the tone. Every one who knows how to play on any instrument knows that some of its tones sound sweeter and are more easily given than others; these are the tones in which the peculiar tone of the instrument and its over-tones sound together. To describe more particularly the natural laws upon which these facts rest would lead us too far away from our present purpose.

THE VOWELS

Every tone in singing usually takes the sound of some vowel. By the greater or less distinctness of one or another of the over-tones, sounding with the fundamental tone, various timbres of the vowel are produced. But certain vowels in certain parts of the scale can be sung far more easily and sweetly than others. The investigation of this fact has taught us that a tone gains in richness when the tone corresponding to the vowel belongs to the over-tones of the fundamental tone. In the human voice, however, the tones favorable to the several vowels do not admit of being precisely determined.

In different languages and dialects the vowels have different shades, and a scarcely perceptible variation, especially in the clearer vowels, is sufficient to cause the over-tones to be heard more or less distinctly. After I had learned, with the kind assistance of Professor Helmholtz, by means of his artificial apparatus for the sharpening of the ear, to find out over-tones and to know their peculiarities, I was soon able, without any artificial help, to discover the vowels favorable to them by the fuller sound of certain tones. In the female voice all tones below the c^1  take the character of *o*. At the c^1

 , *a*, pronounced as in the English word *hall*, sounds the best,

and at $d^{\sharp 1}$ e^1  passes in to *a*, as in *man*, and at f^1

into *a*, as in *may*. With the g^1  the *a* sounds again as in *man*; a^1 b

$\flat^1$ b^1 c^2  are favorable to all the vowels, while d^2 $e\flat^2$

e^2 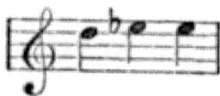 sound best with *e*. After e^2  every tone

takes the coloring of *a*, as in *father*, and sounds well only with this vowel; $b\flat$

^{2} c^3 d^3 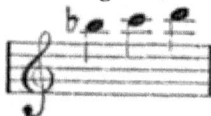 sound again better with *e*. As thus, above e^2 f^2

 all the tones take the coloring of *u* in *father*, so the tones

below c^1  take the timbre of *o*, and the most skilful artists are
not able to sing all the vowels in these tones with equal clearness and purity.
The female voice, therefore, has only a few tones more than an octave, upon
which every one of the vowels can be distinctly sung; and again, all these
tones do not afford an equally sonorous tone with every vowel.

As unfortunately our Song composers do not always keep this fact in view,
as the old Italians did, and since words with the most unfavorable vowels
often underlie the notes, it as often becomes necessary to mingle with the
unfavorable vowel something of the sound (*Klang*) of the vowel properly

belonging to the note; as, for example, in the word "ring" upon f^2

ring , to sing the *i* with a mixture of the sound (*Klang*) of *a*. Artists do this in a way of which they are for the most part unconscious, and which is always unobserved by the hearer. That in every voice there are several tones upon which every vowel sounds well, finds an explanation in an observation of Professor Helmholtz. The ear is attuned to a certain tone, designated as e^4 f^4. To persons with very susceptible nerves these tones are often insupportable, and we often see dogs, whose sense of hearing is especially acute, run howling away when the above e^4 is struck upon a violin, while to other tones they seem wholly insensible. But all the tones which are accompanied by that tone as an over-tone to which the ear is attuned, sound harmonious even with unfavorable vowels.

PARTIAL TONES

But beside the over-tones, which sound with every good, simple sound, there are other *partial tones*, which, like the long-known combination tones, do not usually present themselves to our consciousness. Combination tones were first discovered in 1745 by the organ-builder, *Sorge*. By an act of concentrated attention one hears these tones at the accord of two different tones. They lie always lower than the interval to which they belong, and arise from the meeting of the nodes of vibration of the tones producing the interval. The node of vibration is the name of that place where, after every completed vibration, the sounding body returns to its former position. When, for instance, we give the third c^1 e^1, we hear the c, lying an octave lower than the third, sounding at the same time as a combination tone. For the tone c^1 a string has two vibrations, while in the same space of time e^1 has three. The vibration node of the c^1 will thus, after two vibrations, coincide with the vibration node of the e^1. By the coincidence of these nodes of vibration is produced the number of vibrations requisite for the c below. Besides these combination tones there are summation tones, discovered by Helmholtz, which arise from the vibrations collectively (*Gesammtzahl*) belonging to the above interval, and are higher than the interval. Both kinds of partial tones have again their faint over-tones.

BEATS (DIE SCHWEBUNGEN)

We have explained the movements of the waves of sound by the movements on the surface of water, and we know that, instead of the billows and hollows that we have in the water, the air is condensed and rarefied. We know further that if two different lines of waves run along with one another, their crests and hollows fall together, and their crests become as high again and their hollows as deep again. So two tones from different sources of sound are twice as strong when they are both equally high, and a new tone of the same height added to them will still further increase the sound. But when two agitations of the surface of the water so move that the crests of one fall into the hollows of the other, their movements neutralize each other. The same thing happens in tones when one is not struck until half the vibrations of the preceding tone are concluded. But if the sounding bodies vary in only a small part of a vibration sound, they will be alternately stronger and weaker, and this is termed beats (*Schwebungen*), which are only produced by tones *very near to each other*. Those intervals whose combination and over-tones so fall together that many beats are produced, sound harsh and disagreeable, and we call them dissonances.

Those intervals in which few or no beats occur are called consonances. As the combination or interfering tones, as well as the beats, have importance and interest only in harmonizing several voices, in tuning pianos, as well as in composition in general, and as we have in view in these pages only the culture of single voices, we cannot further enlarge on these discoveries, interesting as they are. According to the purpose of this little work, I introduce only so much of the latest investigations and discoveries as will help to show the prevailing evils of our mode of teaching singing, and, by their practical application to the business of instruction, serve to improve the vocal art. But whoever has an interest in this branch of science will find in the invaluable work of Helmholtz, "*Die Lehre von den Tonempfindungen*," an abundance of most interesting observations and of the most thoroughly scientific illustrations of the theory of music, and of those processes in the domain of tone which we have hitherto always felt, but never understood.

APPLICATION OF THE NATURAL LAWS LYING AT THE FOUNDATION OF MUSICAL SOUNDS TO THE CULTURE OF THE VOICE IN SINGING

The parts of the human voice that generate tones are the membranous vocal ligaments or chords, which are subject to the same natural laws as all sounding bodies; of this we may satisfy ourselves by observing the different registers of the voice by means of the laryngoscope. The lower, stronger tones of both series of the chest register show the ligaments in full vibration, and becoming more strongly stretched with every higher tone. In the second series the glottis appears, by the inaction of the arytenoid cartilages, to be shortened. In the falsetto register the vibrating body is diminished, as only the edges vibrate, while the same processes are repeated as in the chest register by the greater stretching of the ligaments and the shortening of the glottis. The head register, likewise, shows the glottis partly closed, and the vibrating ligaments gradually stretched more and more.

The vocal ligaments are made to vibrate by the air coming from the lungs through the trachea, to which they present resistance. These vibrations are communicated to the air in the mouth and outside, and are felt by the ear as sound.

As the strength of the tone depends upon the amplitude of the waves of sound, they, in their turn, depend upon the structure of the organ of singing, and of the parts of the mouth serving as a sounding-board or resonant apparatus, but, above all, upon the skilful management of the vibrating air. And although a fine timbre of the tones and due skill in increasing the amplitude of the vibrations may cause the voice to appear fuller and stronger, yet it is not in our power, when once the vocal organs have been fully developed, to make a strong voice out of a weak one.

Always to strike the true pitch fully and clearly requires persevering attention, as well from the teacher as from the pupil. And long practice is often required before the intonations become as pure as is indispensably necessary to good singing. For only upon the basis of a full, pure tone is a beautiful timbre (*Klangfarbe*) possible.

But the most important thing in the culture of the voice is the timbre of the tones, for *here it is in our power to form out of a sharp, hard and disagreeable voice, a voice sweet and pleasing.*

We have seen that the timbre is dependent on the forms of the vibrating waves, and the different degrees of strength and number of the over-tones arising from these forms. It has been further shown that the simple round form of the waves of vibration produces the softest, fullest timbre. By this form the fundamental tone is the strongest, and the over-tones are heard ascending to the third octave with decreasing degrees of strength. Such a tone is natural to certain voices. In most cases it must be more or less acquired.

A good tone in singing is formed,

1. By controlling and correctly dividing the air or breath as it is expired;

2. By a correct direction of the vibrating column of air; this is done by the right touch (*Tonansatz*);

And, 3. By a very distinct, quick and elastic *touch*.

THE CONTROL OF THE BREATH

By a too great pressure of the breath, the form of the waves of sound most favorable to a good tone is disturbed. One then hears the high over-tones sounding strongly up to the sixteenth, while the lower over-tones with the fundamental tone sound weak or not at all. Thus the tone takes a shrill, sharp and disagreeable sound when the form of the vibrating waves is more or less disturbed by too great a pressure of air. Too little breath deprives the tone only of its strength, but not of its agreeable sound.

Thus every tone requires for its greatest possible perfection only a certain quantity of breath, which cannot be increased or diminished without injury to its strength in the one case, and its agreeable sound in the other.

In looking carefully through the histories of music, and studying the old Italian schools, we find that it was upon this point—the control and right division of the breathing—that the old masters in the summer of song laid the greatest stress, and this it was to which in teaching they gave the most time and labor. The rules which they followed in this respect, in order to obtain a fine tone, accord perfectly with the results of the latest scientific investigations. And it would be far better for the art of singing if in this respect we had followed the old Italians more faithfully, and not have forsaken so entirely the right way.

According to the old Italian method, which must not be confounded with the modern, the pupil was required at first to breathe just as he was wont to breathe in speaking, and care was taken, by frequent resting-points in the exercises, that the breath should always be renewed at the right time. Accordingly, if the crowding, or pressure, of his breathing was too great, he was required to learn to hold it back. Until the organs were sufficiently practised in the formation of a good tone, and the ear had become familiarized to its sound, pupils were allowed to sing *only piano*. As soon as the pupil had a feeling for a pure tone awakened in him, and could of himself distinguish the finer variations of timbre, he was taught to fill his lungs more and more. But this was to be done, as much as possible, imperceptibly, noiselessly, slowly, and soon enough for him to be able properly to control the quiet breathing in the beginning of a song. Only the sides of the body were in so doing to expand, and breathing with raised chest was allowed only in exceptional cases, as where long passages were to be sung with special passion. For these places, where breath must be taken, there were certain rules which were strictly observed.

After we have learned the natural laws which are applicable in music, and which lie at the basis of a full, rich tone in singing, and that a tone is, strictly speaking, only vibrating air, upon the fine and skilful management of which its beauty and fulness depend, and have considered the careful way in which the old Italians taught the control of the breathing, we cannot but be struck with the rude and negligent manner of using the breath in our present mode of singing.

With some distinguished exceptions, it is now almost universally the practice to require the pupil, as the very first thing, to fill the lungs as full as possible, whereby the chest must be raised. Then the tones must be sung in as strong and long-sustained a manner as possible, in order "to bring out the voice," as the phrase is. He is next told to begin the tones with a full chest *piano*, and slowly swell them to the highest *forte*, and then descend as slowly, in order to learn "to govern the voice." Thus the pupil is always required to sing as strongly as possible, without any special regard to the timbre of the tones, because the timbre is regarded as a peculiarity of different voices, admitting of no change. According to what has been shown in the preceding pages, the present way of using the breath, by which it is supposed that voices are rendered strong and full, only needlessly fatigues the organs, injures the beauty and weakens even the strength of the tones. In the same way we find, especially in the case of tenor voices, that the aim is by greater forcing of the breath to extend the registers beyond their limits. Another fault is often taught: the pupil is required to force with the breath to the due pitch those tones whose pitch is usually struck too low. No voices can ever endure such treatment, and, although the organs may be strong enough to remain sound while under instruction, yet the voice will not continue good, and cannot be of long duration.

We often hear, even in fresh and unsophisticated voices, a hoarse breathing accompanying the tones, as in the case of worn-out voices. This breathing arises when the air, which is exhaled and which rushes into the cavity of the mouth, is not all in vibration, and it escapes along with the vibrating columns of air. It sometimes happens, also, that in the too great pressure of the exhaled air against the glottis, the arytenoid cartilages, near their bases, and sometimes the vocal chords leave a small opening through which the air escapes with a hoarse noise. By keeping back the breath in singing these faults may be corrected. Long-continued singing piano in exercises is, moreover, beneficial in the forming of the voice.[12]

A simple expiration does not indeed suffice for the generation of a full sounding singing tone. There is required a certain force by which the air is sent through the narrow and stretched glottis. But so great an expense of force as people are usually at is not necessary.

The influence of the same stream of air increases in proportion as the breadth of the vibrating ligaments decreases. The tones of the falsetto and head registers, therefore, require far less breath than those of the chest register. The less the quantity of breath expended in these tones, and the easier and more quickly they are produced, the clearer and fuller do they sound. The mechanism of the head tones especially is, as we have seen, so delicate that only a slight excess of breath calls forth the inharmonic over-tones which render the tone sharp and unmusical. In wind instruments the tone can be forced upwards by a greater pressure of air; that is, by more powerful blowing, which appears to be practicable also in those instruments in whose peculiar timbre the highest inharmonic over-tones overpower the others.[13]

Together with the skill and unintermitted attention which this part of instruction in singing requires of the teacher, there are here yet other and peculiar difficulties which he has to meet. In opposition to the earlier and more correct view, it is no longer beauty of tone, but strength of tone, which is considered the chief excellence of a voice. Accustomed to seek the beauty of the voice in its strength, it is attempted, before the time of instruction begins, to sing as strongly as possible from a full chest with the greatest expulsion of breath. Thence it follows, in the superficial way in which the study of the art of singing is at present conducted, that nothing more is commonly required of a teacher than that he should be able to drill his pupil in some pieces of tolerably well conceived vocal music, which the latter must sing as soon as possible in company. A perfect culture of the voice is scarcely any longer expected of an artist. People with a very scanty musical education and voices very poorly trained are regarded as artists if they execute their parts with expression, and trick them out with those clap-traps which never fail to command the applause of the ordinary public.

A conscientious teacher has, therefore, universal opinion against him when he demands a longer time for the education of a voice, and requires of his pupils that they shall practice singing only piano as long as it is necessary.

THE CORRECT TOUCH OF THE VOICE (TONANSATZ)[14]

Having stated the first condition of a good timbre of the tones, we come now to the second—the right direction of the vibrating columns of air. A correct touch of the voice consists in causing the air, brought into vibration by the vocal ligaments, to rebound from immediately above the front upper teeth, where it must be concentrated as much as possible, rebounding thence to form in the mouth continuous vibrations, which are, at the same time, communicated to the external air. The quicker and the more easily these movements take place, and the farther forward in the mouth the vibrating column of air is reflected, the more beautiful, full and telling is the tone. If the air rebounds farther back in the mouth from any part of the roof of the mouth, then the high inharmonic over-tones are prominent, and there arises either one or the other of those hollow, disagreeable colorings of timbre which are known as throat and nasal tones.

That the voice must be brought forward in the mouth—that is, that the air expired in singing should have the above described direction—is now acknowledged as necessary and aimed at by the best teachers. But the reasons why the tones thus sound better are not known. The Germans and the English, in consequence of their accustomed modes of forming sounds in speaking, have, as we shall see hereafter, more rarely than the Italians, a correct disposition of the tones in singing. It is extremely difficult for many persons to accustom themselves to such a direction of the vibrating air-columns. But with the proper means the skilful teacher always gains his end. These means are to let the pupil practice those syllables which he is accustomed, *in his own language*, to form wholly in front of the mouth.

The old Italian masters considered the management or touch of the tone as one of the most important requirements in the perfect cultivation of the voice. Distinctly, lightly, swiftly and elastically must the column of tone, rightly directed, strike the forward part of the mouth, which at the same moment opens widely enough to communicate without delay the quick agitation to the air external to it.

Only by a correct movement of this kind (Ansatz) are those forms of the vibrations obtained in which all the harmonic over-tones belonging to a perfect tone sound together. The quicker, lighter and more distinct this movement of the tone is, the more telling it is, and it may be heard quite strongly, even when it is sung *piano* with a full chorus and orchestra. Upon the occasion of the great Musical Festival in Boston (1869), it was a matter of universal wonder that with the powerful chorus of many thousands of voices, Mad. Parepa-Rosa's tones were heard so distinctly that even at a considerable distance the words were plainly understood. As great artists often find the true and only beautiful unconsciously, so Mad. Parepa-Rosa has a perfectly correct touch, whereby she sets the surrounding air vibrating more rapidly than it is possible for a chorus to do with so many unschooled voices. The sounding waves of the tones which this distinguished singer produced with the correct touch, naturally reached the ear sooner and were earlier felt and taken into the consciousness of the listener than those of the mighty chorus, and thus it was that the music of a single voice kept its significance even with the accompaniment of a multitude of voices.

The great influence of the touch upon the fulness, and especially upon the extent to which tones reach, is again best illustrated by the movements of water. When we press on the surface of water slowly, though with the greatest force, and at the same time touch it in another place quickly and lightly, it is not only far more strongly moved by the quick, light touch, but the waves which are produced spread themselves out more rapidly, and run more swiftly over the surface, than those of the slower and more powerful pressure.

As the form of the vibrations necessary to a perfect tone in singing depends mainly upon a right management of tone, it is self-evident that here the greatest care should be taken in teaching vocal music. Here is one of the most difficult tasks for the teacher, and great perseverance and much practice are required of the pupil. But when once a right production of tone has become a habit, so that with every tone all the harmonic over-tones sound, and more breath is then allowed to stream forth immediately after the quick, light rebound of the vibrating column of tone, the vibrations enlarge without changing their form, and so only the strongest, fullest, most beautiful tone possible is obtained. But a touch can only be learned by imitation. We can no more describe the fine shades of tone than of color. And no art, least of all the art of singing, can be learned from books alone.

FORMATION OF VOWELS AND CONSONANTS

The sound of the vowels depends, as we have seen, upon whether one or another of the over-tones takes precedence in sound. But the conditions by which the formation of the vowels is determined lie in the form of the cavity of the mouth, and of the contraction of the same in some one place or another during expiration. These places are different in different languages and dialects. They are among the English, Germans and French farthest back in sounding *a*, as in *father*; farther forward in *a*, as in *may*, *o*, *e*, in the order in which they are here placed; and farther front in the German *u* (*oo*).

The length of the cavity of the mouth is the greatest in sounding *oo*, the least in *e*, intermediate in *a*. In the pure, clear *a*, as in *may*, or *e* of the Germans, the cavity is the narrowest. Hence, to form a tone on this vowel is very difficult, and it is the only vowel whose pure pronunciation must be sacrificed to the tone. Good tones can be formed on this vowel when in both series of the chest register there is mingled with it the sound of the German *ö*, pronounced in English nearly like the vowel in *bird*, and in the higher registers the sound of the *e*—that is, of the German *i*. The cavity of the mouth is thus somewhat broadened, and the tone gains more room for its development.

The Swiss form the *o* and *u* like the *a* in *father*, broadest at the back of the mouth, and the *e* broadest towards the front. But the Italians form no vowel as far front as their clear sounding beautiful *a*, as in *father*; and probably because the *a* in the Italian language sounds broadest and most distinctly, Italian wagoners drive their beasts with the shout of *a! a!* while the Germans use for the same purpose, *hü! huo!* and the Swiss, *hipp!* One can only approximate an imitation of the Italian *a* by uttering it in connection with consonants coming rapidly, as in *pfa*, *bra*, and in as short and rapid a manner as possible.

The old Italian masters naturally found their beautiful *a* most favorable to the formation of a good tone in singing; and thus it has been adopted by other nations. But here is the very reason why a tone free from badly sounding colorings is so rarely heard. We have blindly imitated the Italians, without considering the different modes of forming the vowels in different languages and nations, and that the Italian *a* is a vowel entirely different from the German and the similarly sounding English *a*. Its correct sound is learned by those to whom it is not vernacular only with difficulty.

As the vowels are differently formed in different languages, so is it also with the consonants. The North Germans form the letter *r* with the soft palate, which is made to vibrate by the exhalation of the breath. The South Germans, Russians and Italians form the *r* by the vibration of the tip of the tongue. It is only this mode of forming the *r* which is to be used in singing, and must be learned by those who do not usually form it thus. This is sometimes rather difficult, but it can be done by repeating frequently and rapidly, one after the other, the syllables *hede, hedo*, or *ede, edo*. In this way the tongue gets accustomed to the right position and motion, which it by-and-by learns rapidly enough for the formation of the rolling *r*.

The Italians, likewise, form the *l* with the tip of the tongue, the Germans and English mostly with the side edges of the tongue. With some attention one can, by feeling, find out in his own organ the place for the formation of the different vowels and consonants, and an ear accustomed to delicate differences of tone will perceive the right place in others.

But in teaching, the example of the wagoners must be followed, and as these people have found out the most appropriate vowels and syllables whereby to make themselves understood by their animals, we must choose what is best fitting to the formation of tone in singing.

Long before I found the scientific reason of this mode of proceeding, my attention was called by Frederic Wiek, in Dresden, to the fact that a fine tone can be most quickly attained by practising in the beginning upon the syllables *sü, soo*, or *dü, doo*, and by not passing to the other vowels until one is accustomed to produce tones in the front of the mouth. These syllables are naturally spoken by the Germans and the English in the front part of the mouth. The *s* is formed with the lips apart, while the air is blown through the upper teeth; it thus assists one, united with *u* (*oo*), to direct the tone forwards. But because in the *u* the lips are almost closed, care must be taken that, within the lips, the teeth are far enough apart. The cavity of the mouth must be large enough to allow of the largest possible wave of sound, since upon the size of that, as we know, the strength of the tone depends. When the pupil, after some practice, has learned to give the right direction to the stream of sound, he must be required gradually to form the other vowels like the *soo* in the front part of the mouth, passing from this syllable immediately to the other vowels, as, for example, *soo-a, soo-o, soo-e, soo-o-e-ah*, &c. Only care must be taken that the course of the air preserves its right direction.

Solmisation, also, i. e., naming the tones, *c, d, e, f, g, a, b*, by the syllables *do, re, mi, fa, sol, la, si*, assists a good touch when the pupil employs it in the more rapid exercises.

There is no fixed rule that can be laid down in regard to the necessary opening of the mouth and its position. The structure of the palate and the form of the jaw, and the position of the teeth, lips, &c., vary in different persons. The ear of the teacher must alone determine what position of those several parts will best secure a good timbre. But in every case, for the highest tones of the voice the widest possible opening of the mouth is necessary, and even when, in the formation of the vowels, the lips have to be brought nearer to each other, yet the teeth within must be kept apart, that the cavity of the mouth may remain large enough.

Wind instruments show the influence which the orifice and breadth of the bell has upon the strength of the tone. In the human voice the mouth occupies the place of the bell.

We have already made the remark, in speaking of the different registers, that in the chest tones the position of the larynx is lowered. The cavity of the mouth, then, is naturally lengthened, and hence a moderate opening of the mouth, so that, in singing the notes of the low chest register, the teeth are a thumb's breadth apart, suffices for a good tone. The second chest register requires the slightest opening of the mouth. It is enough if one can press a finger between the teeth. With the high falsetto and head tones the cavity of the mouth is always shorter and narrower towards the back, but as the tones ascend, it must be always broader in front. In singing the first falsetto register, the teeth should be about the breadth of the thumb apart; in the second falsetto register, two fingers apart; and in the head register, the mouth must be open as far as possible. But precise rules cannot here be given. I have observed, however, that in thin voices a too broad opening of the mouth in the middle tones of the voice favors the high over-tones more than the fundamental tone, and the tones are thus flat and wanting in timbre.

Lips too thick and stiff sometimes injure the timbre of the tone; they are often the cause of a veiled, muffled timbre, acting like dampers and rendering a part of the over-tones inaudible. In such cases, as soon as he has become accustomed to a correct direction of the column of tone, the pupil should keep the lips as close to the teeth as possible, and draw back somewhat the corners of the mouth.

The tongue also is not infrequently a hindrance to the formation of a good tone, especially when the pupils have not been taught early enough to open their mouths sufficiently wide. When the high tones are to be produced, which require much room in the forward part of the mouth, the tongue is usually drawn back and raised, in order to make the necessary room within the lower front teeth. This, again, is a habit difficult to be broken, and care must be taken that the lower front teeth are lightly touched by the tip of the tongue in singing, in order that the tongue may be accustomed to a natural position. But this is most easily attained when the tongue is at the first kept occupied as much as possible by quick exercises with the syllables of solmisation, or by practising tones in slow time upon syllables beginning with consonants formed by the tip of the tongue. As in pronouncing the German *Sch* the tongue presses the teeth all around with its outer edge, syllables formed with these consonants serve excellently well to accustom the tongue to a quiet, correct position.

FLEXIBILITY OF VOICE

We hear it continually said that it requires a special natural gift to acquire a certain ease and flexibility of voice, and that this natural gift is peculiar to the Italians. But the flexibility of the voice depends upon a physiologico-physical process of the organ of tone, which, among the Italians, goes on in their common speech, and hence is more easily transferred by them to their singing. In trills, roulades, turns, and all tones quickly succeeding one another, the breath must set the vocal chords vibrating in quick, short pulses. The little time used by the breath between these rapidly succeeding pulses to retreat, in order to give another pulse, suffices perfectly to produce easily and quickly the position of the glottis requisite for a higher or lower tone. In order, between the pulses, to give room to the retreating breath, the windpipe expands laterally, whereby the larynx is always somewhat drawn down, in order, with the next pulse of the breath, to take again its former place. This rising and lowering of the larynx can be seen plainly outside the throat, and it can be seen also whether the movement goes on rightly. Upon the degree of rapidity with which this movement goes on depends the greater or less flexibility of the voice.

But when the breath in exhaling presses in regularly increasing strength against the vocal chords, and one wishes to pass quickly to a higher tone and back again, as is required in trills, while the aerial stream continues to flow on with unintermitted force, it is evident that the changed movement of the glottis, even within the limits of a register, demands more time and muscular force than a beautiful trill or run admits of. But at the same time the limits of the tones become, by the uninterrupted stream of air, obliterated, and embellishments sung in this way, with unmoved larynx, indistinct. But ornamentation is now practised only in this latter way, and if pupils do not naturally move their throats correctly, the gift of flexibility is denied them.

A quite prevalent and likewise incorrect way of using the throat is moving the epiglottis with the larynx, which renders the formation of a clear, pure tone impossible, and *fioriuri* sung in this way are limp and indistinct. The only correct movement shows itself very plainly externally, so that with the tolerably strong movement of the larynx up and down, there can be seen also a slighter movement of the windpipe far below in the neck, about the breadth of two fingers above the breast-bone. The mouth and tongue, however, must be perfectly quiet.

But the cultivation of vocal flexibility in singing is the easiest and most grateful part of the education of the voice, for with ordinary industry on the part of the pupil results are here obtained most speedily. In the very first lessons I teach my pupils the motions of the vocal organ in trills, and if they do not learn them by imitation, I give them simple exercises on the syllable *koo* to practice for a while. The *k* is produced by a pulse of the breath, and the *oo* is, as we have seen, the best vowel sound with which to direct the breath as it is expired. Thus, by singing *staccato* the syllable *koo*, slowly at first and gradually quicker, with a movement of the larynx and windpipe that is both seen and felt; and with the tongue and lips at rest and motionless, the right movement is given to the organ in trills and all other embellishments, and by continued practice the movement becomes more rapid. Those who need to be taught this movement must never practice continuously for any length of time, for we must avoid fatiguing the organs. When pupils have become accustomed, by rapidly singing the syllable *koo* on each tone of the trill, to the movement of the larynx, then they can practice upon another syllable, and in the following way: Let the trill be at first always sung *piano*, with an accenting of the higher tone every time and a gradual increasing of the rapidity thus:

; also in half and whole tones, and then in minor thirds. But the most beautiful trill will be formed by practising triplets in the compass of a whole tone, then of a minor third, major third, fourth, etc., by which first the upper, then the lower tone is accented:

. The mouth, however, in this exercise must continue immovably open, and the tongue also must lie perfectly still, touching the lower front teeth, for only in this way can one be sure of not moving the epiglottis. Although this is difficult at first, yet the syllable *ku* (koo) may be sung in this way. Thus, with sufficient practice, any one may acquire a perfect flexibility of voice. When the pupils can make the trill easily upon the middle tones, in which in the beginning exercises must be practised, let them practice also upon the higher and lower tones of the voice. If the trill takes place at the transition of two registers, then both the tones must be formed upon the higher of the two, as in an exchange of registers the glottis requires more time than a good trill admits of.

Rapid runs downwards are easily executed correctly when care is taken that with every tone the same movement is made as in the case of trills, and the breath is kept back as much as possible. Voices wanting in flexibility may soon acquire the desired quality by singing every tone *piano* upon the syllable *koo*.

Ascending runs can properly be taught only when the descending have been correctly sung, for, in opposition to the former, every tone of the latter must be formed by a light impulse with increased breath. The softer the piano in which the pupil practises, and the more loose the consequent movement of the larynx, the more distinctly and the more purely will the pupil gradually execute these embellishments.

Intelligible as these movements are in practice, it is difficult to describe them. To be able to make all ornaments in singing beautifully and easily requires long practice, for in a thoroughly artistic piece of vocal music it is essential, as the great artist *Schröder-Devrient* said, that all the notes of ornamentation (*Coloratur*) should be like a string of pearls on black velvet, each distinct in itself, round and beautiful, and yet so connected with the rest in one whole that no gap is discernible. Carefully and correctly directed exercises in ornamentation are in the highest degree necessary to the formation of tone; they tire the voice far less than sustained notes, and accustom it to an exact enunciation of the tones. But because persevering practice is necessary to the cultivation of vocal flexibility, the teaching of this is to be begun at the very first; and not until later, when the voice is habituated to a right touch and to a perfectly clear tone, is the pupil to be given those favorite exercises with long-sustained notes, which are sung with one continuous breath. That we so rarely meet with clear vocal fluency is again owing to our mode of teaching. We do not seek to cultivate formation of tone and fluency at the same time. Oftentimes it is only after years spent in singing sustained tones that ornaments are allowed to be practised, and then, instead of using as little breath as possible, the flexibility of the larynx is hindered by singing too powerfully with full chest and unintermitted crowding of the breath. Without denying that in regard to vocal flexibility different individuals and nations may be variously gifted, it is nevertheless certain that *with due practice every one may acquire more or less of vocal fluency.*

Frederick Wiek has composed for his pupils a large number of simple exercises, in which all kinds of ornaments are introduced, and which at the same time are so melodious that they easily catch the ear. They mostly comprise only a few tones, at the most an octave, and are sung in half tones, ascending in different keys. Next to these exercises come, as highly adapted to the culture of vocal flexibility, the solfeggi of *Mieksch, Mazzoni, Rossini, Crescentini,* &c. There is, indeed, no want of excellent exercises and solfeggi. Their use, however, depends upon the way in which the teacher requires them to be practised. Notwithstanding the abundance of these exercises, I have always found it necessary to prepare special ones for my pupils, as every voice requires peculiar treatment and guidance.[15] In every pupil peculiar faults are to be overcome and peculiar qualities come into play, and the vocal organ shows as many differences as the human face. But the right way is sure to be found when the irreversible laws of nature, which lie at the foundation of our art, are once recognized. The practical advantages of this knowledge the singer, like every other artist, must endeavor to secure orally, that is, by sound instruction. Ornamentation, however, can become distinct and clear only by uniting these with a distinct, pure touch, as we have already endeavored to describe, when, with the beginning of the tone, the pitch is struck lightly, quickly, distinctly, elastically, with certainty and perfect correctness. But as it is by no means easy to introduce a tone quickly and correctly, so that it will sound equally pure from the first, this flexibility is extremely rare among our singers. Instead of it, the most hateful mannerisms have stolen into practice; the tone is struck too low, and forced up by an increase of breath, or the tones are so drawled one into another that one cannot tell where they begin or where they cease. Impure intonation is much more disagreeable in the high tones than in the low. This is quite natural; for when, for example, the low c is sung one-tenth too low or too high, then it will cause an octave higher twice as many vibrations, and two octaves higher four times as many, and these in proportion to their number produce a more intense effect. In the higher registers of the tones little discords (*Verstimmungen*) call forth a much larger number of beats (which are not to be confounded with vibrations) than in the lower, and thus the impurity of the musical intervals is felt much more strongly. Purity in the art of singing is, however, such a primal condition of its beauty, that a piece of music purely executed, even by a weak and slightly-cultivated voice, always sounds agreeably, while the most sonorous and practised voice offends the hearer when it is out of tune or forced upwards. The training of our singers by pianos, as they are now tuned, by equal temperament, is altogether unsatisfactory. The singer who practises with the piano has no safe principle by which he can measure the height of his tones with any exactness. But persons of good musical talent, made aware of this disadvantage by a competent teacher, and practising accordingly, can nevertheless overcome this difficulty caused by our present method of tuning, and learn to sing correctly and purely.

Until the seventeenth century, singers were drilled by the monochord, for which *Zarlino*, in the middle of the sixteenth century, re-introduced the correct, natural tuning. The drilling of singers was conducted at that time with a care of which we have now no idea. The church music of the fifteenth and sixteenth centuries is arranged upon the purest consonant chords, depending upon this for its whole effect, which would naturally be injured if not executed with perfect purity. Our opera singers now-a-days are seldom able to sing without accompaniment a composition for several voices so purely that its whole beauty is felt; the accord almost always sounds sharp and somewhat uncertain, and therefore cannot satisfy a really musical ear.

SPEECH

The vowels and consonants are, in speaking, produced by certain noises (*Geräusche*), which in singing sound together with the tone. These sounds are produced by local diminutions of the cavity of the mouth, or by the opening or closing of the lips and teeth, as well as by movements of the tip of the tongue, &c., while a single pulse of the air passes through the tolerably wide open glottis and through the cavity of the mouth without regular vibrations. For the air rushes more directly out of the mouth in speaking than in singing. Of this we may be easily convinced by holding a feather before the mouth; it will show far more motion in speaking than in correct singing. If, in speaking, people would take pains to form the vowels in the front of the mouth—a habit so necessary in singing, and which is easily acquired by practice—our common speech would be much more melodious, far-sounding, and less strained. We see the truth of this when we hear words called out from a height and from a distance; the different consonants then mostly disappear, excepting the *m* and *n*, which are formed mostly in the front of the mouth. The vowels, on the other hand, are more or less plainly heard, according to the places in the mouth where they are formed. Certain it is that for the beauty of our common speech, the resonance of the cavity of the mouth peculiar to each vowel may be rendered available. A singing tone in speaking is very disagreeable. Every one who is not used to it, finds the singing dialect of Saxony in the highest degree offensive and unpleasant. Nevertheless, a more attentive observation soon teaches us that behind the noise which characterizes the several sounds in language, a timbre is heard similar to the tone in singing, and in various instances there occur regular musical intervals, as at the end of a sentence or in the special accentuation of single words. Thus, at the conclusion of an affirmative sentence the voice usually falls about a fourth from the medium pitch, and at the end of an interrogatory sentence rises about a fifth above the usual speaking tone. Words specially accented are usually a tone higher than the rest, &c. In public speaking and in dramatic representations these variations of sound are more numerous and complicated, and the inventor of the modern Recitative, *Jacob Perri*, even declares that he formed it by imitating in singing these variations of sound, in order to restore again the declamation of the ancient tragedians.[16]

Tedious and intolerable as it is to hear so much sing-song in common speech, it is equally wearisome when people drone on always in a dry speaking tone at the same pitch, without ever letting the voice rise or fall. The most interesting matter thus delivered will lull the hearer to sleep. It cannot be denied that a rich field is here offered for farther scientific observation, and those natural laws which lie at the foundation of the art of singing may certainly be applied with advantage to the perfecting of the mode of speaking, especially in those who have to speak in public.[17]

To extend these remarks any farther does not come within our present purpose, which is concerned exclusively with the voice in singing and its cultivation. For this reason I leave unnoticed many most interesting phenomena relating to music in general, but not particularly to the culture of the voice, although they are of the deepest interest to the educated musician.

---

7 Tyndall.

---

8 The concert pitch in different places and at different periods has undergone great changes. The Grand Opera in Paris in the year 1700 established 404 vibrations to a second as the concert pitch of a^1, which gradually rose higher, as the wind instruments became more perfect and had a more important part assigned them in concerted music, until 1858 it had attained the height of 448 vibrations in a second. In this same year (1858) at Berlin and St. Petersburg it reached its greatest height—451½ vibrations in the second. In Mozart's time, in Vienna, it had only 422 and 428 vibrations.

---

9 As long as melody alone was aimed at in music, and was accompanied only by octaves, the tones preserved their natural purity. But with the rise of harmony (the accord of different tones) there was rendered necessary a more regular system, to which the purity of the tones was sacrificed.

---

10 "It is not possible to sound a stretched string as a whole without at the same time causing to a greater or less extent its subdivision; that is to say, superposed upon the vibrations of the string we have always, in a greater or less degree, the vibrations of its aliquot parts. The higher notes produced by these latter vibrations are called the *harmonics* of the string. And so it is with other sounding bodies; we have, in all cases, a co-existence of vibrations. Higher tones mingle with the fundamental tone, and it is their intermixture which determines what, for want of a better term, we call the *quality* of the sound. The French call it *timbre*, and the Germans call it *Klangfarbe*. It is this union of high and low tones that enables us to distinguish one musical instrument from another. A clarionet and a violin, for example, though tuned to the same fundamental note, are not confounded...."

"All bodies and instruments, then, employed for producing musical sounds, emit, besides their fundamental tones, tones due to higher order of vibrations. The Germans embrace all such sounds under the general term *Obertöne*. I think it will be an advantage if we, in England, adopt the term *overtones*, as the equivalent of the term employed in Germany. One has occasion to envy the power of the German language to adapt itself to requirements of this nature. The term *Klangfarbe*, for example, employed by Helmholtz, is exceedingly expressive, and we need its equivalent also. You know that color depends upon rapidity of vibrations—that blue light bears to red the same relation that a high tone does to a low one. A simple color has but one rate of vibration, and it may be regarded as the analogue of a simple tone in music. A *tone*, then, may be defined as the product of a vibration which cannot be decomposed into more simple ones. A compound color, on the contrary, is produced by the admixture of two or more simple ones; and an assemblage of tones, such, as we obtain when the fundamental tone and the harmonics of a string sound together, is called by the Germans a *Klang*. May we not employ the English word *clang* to denote the same thing, and thus give the term a precise scientific meaning akin to its popular one? And may we not, like Helmholtz, add the word *color* or *tint* to denote the character of the clang, using the term *clang-tint* as the equivalent of *Klangfarbe?*" (*Sound: A course of Lectures delivered at the Royal Institution of Great Britain by John Tyndall, LL.D., F. R. S., Professor of Nat. Phil. in the Royal Institution and in the Royal School of Mines. English edition, pp. 116–118.*)—TR.

---

11 As to the characteristic sounds of the different keys, the views of musicians are to the present day divided. Many even of our most eminent theorists, as Hauptmann, for example, in Leipsig, have maintained that all keys (*Tonarten*) are only transpositions of one major and minor key, and that like musical effects may be produced with one as well as with the other. The majority of musicians are, however, of the opinion that each key has its peculiar character, and that by transposition into another key the musical effect is changed. My son, Carl Seiler, has discovered that each key has its own peculiar, prominent over-tones, which determine its distinctive character. A table of all the keys (*Tonarten*), in which the prominent over-tones of each are given, shows also that the mutual relation of the keys (*Tonarten*) is elucidated by these over-tones. And thus again scientific investigation confirms what the founders of the theory of music, with their sound sense for the beautiful, recognized as correct.

---

12 The position of the body in singing must be such as in no way to interfere with the easy drawing of the breath. One sings most easily standing as erect

as possible, quiet and unconstrained, the chest somewhat projected, the body slightly drawn in, and the hands folded.

---

13 It was instruments of this class—trumpets, horns, bugles, etc.—in whose timbre the highest inharmonic over-tones overpower all the rest, that were painfully offensive to the exquisite musical organization of Mozart from his earliest childhood.

---

14 It is all but impossible to give an idea of what is meant by *Tonansatz*, without a practical illustration. It is that striking of the note or the air corresponding to the touch in piano-playing.

---

15 A selection of such exercises, prepared by the present writer, has recently been published by Mr. O. Ditson in Boston, and also two books of old Italian solfeggi from Mieksch and Mazzoni, arranged to the present pitch.

---

16 According to *Boethius*, the *lyra*, which was used by the Greeks to accompany declamation, embraced, in the tuning of its strings, the principal intervals used in speaking.

---

17 Since the appearance of this book I have often been consulted by persons whose calling required them to speak in public, and whose vocal organs were no longer competent thereto. Here also I have found in most cases that there was an incorrect use of the registers, and that men especially form the lowest sounds with that forced enlarging of the windpipe already mentioned (that is, with the so-called *Strohbassregister*). Many have probably fallen into this unnatural and exhausting manner by attempting to speak or to sing loudly. Together with the incorrect use of the registers, there is also an incorrect management (*Leitung*) of the vibrating air, which so often renders speaking so difficult to public speakers. As, when the voice is not wholly directed to the front of the mouth, it does not move the external air quickly enough and so does not reach far, the speaker commonly tries to help himself by a greater expenditure of force. Misled by false views, speakers usually attempt by a great waste of breath and by exertion alone to produce an effect which can be realized only by skilful management of the most delicate and easily moved of all things, the air.

IV
THE ÆSTHETIC VIEW
OF THE ART OF SINGING

HAVING treated, in the two preceding divisions of this book, of the physiological and physical laws lying at the basis of singing tones, and of their practical application to the formation of the voice, we come now to the better known—the æsthetic—part of our task.

The reader will bear in mind that as, in the preceding sections, our attention has been confined to what directly relates to the culture of the voice in singing, notwithstanding the strong temptation to transcend the limits which our present design prescribes, so in this section also the same purpose is kept in view, and it is not to be regarded as treating of the æsthetics of music in general.

Hitherto we have had to do with fixed, irreversible laws, which are to be implicitly followed in order to render singing as perfect as possible. We have seen how the decline of the art of singing had to follow as a necessary consequence the non-observance of these laws. In speaking thus far of the agreeable and the disagreeable, of the beautiful and its opposite, we have had no reference to artistic feeling. We have been concerned only with direct sensuous pleasure or pain, not with æsthetic beauty. We have been occupied thus far with the *technique* of our art—the form. But with the animating spirit of this form, the *æsthetic*, we enter upon a broader field, which, dependent upon purely psychological reasons (*Motiven*), may undergo a change, either from the general progress of mankind or from the culture of the practised artist. Thus, although from Aristotle down to Lessing and our own times the principles of beauty in all the arts are the same, yet every period, in which art has nourished, has produced works, various indeed, and corresponding to the spirit of the age, works, which, however, notwithstanding all differences, have still conformed to the demands of the principles of beauty. Thus, in architecture, sculpture, painting, music, &c., there are different styles of art, every one of which, however, has its justification and its peculiar beauty. We are not, therefore, to judge these different styles of art by the taste and ideas (*Auffassung*) of the present, but by the character of the times that produced them. Although the mode of thinking may vary in accordance with the different stages of culture of individuals and mankind, there are, nevertheless, certain principles of beauty which all nature announces.

By beauty we understand the highest perfection of the single parts in a perfectly represented whole, and the most intimate union of the ideal with the material, i. e., of the spiritual with the formal, which must have as its basis a certain proportion and order in the position of the several parts as well as in their relation to the whole work. In the perception of the beautiful, everything must tend to awaken the feeling of repose and pleasure; and the more susceptible we are of the impression of the beautiful, the more shall we be disturbed by defects, even the least, in any work of art. The pleasure which we take in any work of art, which, however faultless in certain respects, shows any glaring defect, is greatly abridged. The ugly spot will absorb our attention and destroy the pure enjoyment of its beauty, and still more disagreeable will be the effect if the different *parts*, otherwise beautifully shaped, are thrown out of their due symmetry and proportion. In the successive arts, as music, the dramatic art, &c., proportion (*Maassvolle*) is an essential condition of beauty, more than in the simultaneous arts; and an artist whose *technique* is altogether perfect, and who can succeed in reproducing every emotion of the mind in his work, is a true artist only when he never transgresses by an excess of passion the fine boundary lines of beauty.

It is given to only a very few to recognize at once the high and beautiful in art. In most the sense of the beautiful awakens only with a riper spiritual development. It is thus the fruit of a higher stage of culture. To children and persons wholly uneducated a brightly painted picture-book is more beautiful than the Dresden Madonna, that great masterpiece of painting. And most people take greater pleasure in a waltz by *Strauss* or *Lanner* than in a symphony by Beethoven or Mozart. Beauty depends upon principles, i. e., rules and laws, which are founded in the nature of the human reason. The appreciation, therefore, of beauty accompanies the development in man of his reason.

Music, above all the other arts, finds the earliest and most universal recognition, and almost every one listens to it with pleasure. Helmholtz says that music is much more intimately related to our sensations than all the other arts put together. Tones touch the ear and are instantly felt to be agreeable or disagreeable, while the impressions of painting, poetry, &c., upon our senses must be brought to our consciousness, and be judged of there by comparison. But it is not only through the direct effect of tones, as it appears to me, but more through the life (*Belebung*) which animates it, that music comes so close to us, and is so natural and near of kin to us. That must needs be the most interior of the arts whose office it is to express the various moods of the human soul in their tenderest and most secret fluctuations. The incorporeal material of tone is far better fitted to express these different moods (*Stimmungen*) than it is possible for poetry to do. Peculiar, definite feelings it cannot, indeed, distinctly denote without the help of poetry. But it is this very indefiniteness that enables music so to insinuate itself into the soul of the hearer that the tones heard seem to be the expression of his own feelings, and not those of another. Hence it is that music, in its whole nature, acts beneficently and soothingly, because its ruling principle is always a striving after repose, after a rest in *consonances*, just as this is the innermost aim and struggle of our own life. In the other arts this is much less the case. Aristotle, in his twenty-seventh and twenty-ninth problems, distinguishes the influences of music as the expression of tones of feeling (*Stimmungen*), and not of definite feelings. And *Brendel*, who, in his history of music, holds to the order among the arts received by the Greeks, by which architecture takes the lowest place, then sculpture, painting, music, and, lastly, as the highest of the arts, poetry, remarks, that "Music, by virtue of its power to express the most delicate shades of sentiment, would certainly take the highest rank were it more definite." It has always been attempted to extend the boundaries of music by calling in the assistance of painting and poetry. Haydn, Mozart, Schubert, etc., have imitated in their compositions the singing of birds, the rippling of water, storms, &c. And now our modern musicians of the future endeavor to express in tones definite thoughts and feelings, imagining that here a new epoch in art is to open. But these new compositions always require elaborate explanations. Music until now, at least, has not yet given up its ethereal, indefinite character.[18]

It is essential to the full effect of a work of art that the artist should create it, and the hearer or beholder should enjoy it, without thinking of the rules and laws of beauty. A work of art must act immediately upon the feelings; it must appear to be spontaneous, and must be felt without reference to any aim or plan. What is æsthetically beautiful pleases a cultivated taste at once without any reflex consideration. But when, by the help of the understanding, we seek to account for the harmony and perfection of the several parts, and find by more searching study that the work is in conformity to the laws of reason, our enjoyment will naturally be enhanced. But this study must always come as a consequence of the first effect upon the soul, otherwise all effect is wanting. The *unconscious* enjoyment of the legitimate in art is the first condition of the influence of the beautiful upon the soul. The happy, elevated feeling which all works of art immediately awaken in us is thus only an unconscious recognition of the reasonable, the harmonious, the symmetrical. But this unconscious impression is instantly disturbed by any, the least imperfection, before we perceive where and in what it consists, for the human mind is not able fully and at once to examine a production of art in its entirety to its minutest parts.

An artist must, therefore, be esteemed according as his works excite and ravish the hearers or beholders without their knowing why, and he stands all the higher the simpler and the more naturally—i. e., the more *unconsciously*—this takes place.

In order to reach such a height, and to be able to act upon the souls of men with an elevating and informing power, it is first of all necessary that an artist should cultivate the form, or the *technique*, of his art to its greatest possible perfection, and have such perfect command of it, that the practical application of it is as natural to him as to breathe. *For empty and dead as all technical knowledge is unless it is animated with a soul, yet no product of art æsthetically beautiful is possible without a perfect technique.*

But the culture of the *technique* in the art of singing requires a special faculty in the teacher, and, together with the finest power of observation, an ear, which not only perceives the purity of the tone, whether high or low, but feels also the direction of the aerial column, the too much or too little of the breath, the coloring of the timbre, &c. An æsthetically artistic education demands likewise that the singer should have the highest general culture. As soon as the technical education has advanced so far that it no longer makes any demand upon the attention of the learner, the infusion of life and soul into the singing must be begun. The teacher must then be so filled with the spirit of his art that he shall be able so to inspire his pupils that, forgetting themselves, they may be absorbed in the high ideal work of their art, and regard their well-trained voices simply as expressing the noblest and most varied sentiments (*Stimmungen*). And on this account a teacher should seek to act upon the souls of his pupils, and awaken in them above all things a feeling for the high and the noble, that they may be able to find the correct mode of expressing it in singing. It is a very hard but not impossible work to educate true artists, who, penetrated with faith in the high worth of their art, shall fulfil its aim by exercising a refreshing and elevating influence upon their fellow-men. But, in order to be able to form true artists, a teacher must be devoted without intermission to his own culture, scientific and general; must strive with pleasure, and love, and inspiration to accomplish the high work of his calling, and make the severest demands upon himself, before he can expect anything great of his pupils.

Having spoken of those parts of the *technique* of the art of singing which rest upon impregnable natural laws, such as the registers of the voice, the formation of tones in regard to strength, pitch, and timbre, &c., let us consider more closely those other parts of the *technique* which rest upon psychological, i. e., æsthetic principles (*Motiven*). To these belong *Rhythm, Correct understanding of the Tempo, Composition, Execution, that is, the delivery of the sentiment of the composition, and the aids thereto.*

RHYTHM

To the principles of beauty belong, above all things, order and regularity. In music this order consists in measures of time. All measurement by time, even the scientific, depends upon rhythmic, regularly returning results, as in the revolutions of the earth, of the moon, and in the vibrations of the pendulum, &c. Thus, by the regular interchange of accented and unaccented sounds in music and poetry, we obtain the rhythm of the work.

But while in poetry the structure of verse serves only to reduce to artistic order the external accidents of expression by language, rhythm is not only the external measure of time in music, but it belongs to the innermost nature of its power of expression, giving to music its distinctive character. There is, therefore, a finer and much more various culture of rhythm necessary in music than in poetry. Here rhythm determines not only the time, how long a note is to be maintained, and how many notes fall within a certain space of time, but it also distinguishes those notes which are to be sung with more or less emphasis.

We know that in a bar of . $\frac{2}{4}$ time the first beat must be more accented than the second; in a bar of $\frac{4}{4}$ time the rhythmical accent falls upon the first and third beats; in a bar of $\frac{3}{4}$ and $\frac{3}{8}$ time only upon the first; and in $\frac{6}{8}$ upon the first and fourth. This rhythmical accentuation must become a second nature to the learner before he can express any particular sentiment in a piece of music, and therefore he must be early practised in it. Rhythmical accentuation can always be employed very differently according to the character (*Stimmung*) of a composition, and the most different effects in expression are thus produced. One can, by a greater or less degree of strength, or by a sudden impulse of the breath, change the accent, as well as by a slight retardation of the note. Also, by transferring the accent to those notes naturally not accented, that is, in the $\frac{2}{4}$ time to the second beat, or to the second half of the first, by so-called *syncopes*, the whole character of a piece is changed. In musical passages in which many notes come upon one beat and the character of which is light and pleasing, a peculiar charm is produced when several rhythmical accents are made upon the same beat, and likewise in slow passages the swelling of the tone upon the accented note is very pleasing. Let the same phrase in a song be sung with different rhythmical accents, and we may easily see how such changes will give the passage quite another character.

The old Italian singers understood to a remarkable degree the use of rhythm in the execution of vocal music. But the poetical rhythm of the words accompanying the voice gives to the singer a guide, reference to which shows him at least how and where he may employ the nicer shades of musical rhythm.

CORRECT UNDERSTANDING OF THE TEMPO

To give the pupil the feeling for the correct tempo of a composition is more difficult than to teach him to understand rhythm. Our best musicians, whose merits deserve the fullest acknowledgment, often fail here, making the tempo of a piece of music either too slow or too quick, and so weakening its whole effect. This happens especially with the old compositions which preceded the introduction of the metronome. The old Italian vocal compositions are in this respect treated the worst by our musicians, who belong to the strictly classical school. The character of these pieces is prevailingly sentimental, and the *tempi* were not so quick then as now. If a piece thus composed in slow time is set, without reference to its sentiment, to the quickest possible tempo, it becomes ordinary and vulgar in character; the most beautiful adagio may in this way be degraded to a street-ballad. The songs of our modern composers have to be sung to a quicker tempo than that to which they are set, or they are tedious and wearisome. This is particularly the case with the compositions of Schubert, and the whole effect of his beautiful songs is often ruined by a degree more or less too rapid. Singing too slowly, or in false tempo, is now-a-days a very prevalent fault. And yet the singer has in the words a surer guide than is granted to the instrumental performer. Therefore, by well considering these and getting them by heart without the music, as if they were the outpouring of his own feelings, he will be most likely to strike the correct tempo in singing them. In this way many of our recent favorite songs gain a somewhat fresher tempo than that at which they are usually sung. The choice of the time, being dependent upon the taste of the artist, requires special attention and study.

Although the tempo is usually indicated by some designation, as, for example, allegro, adagio, &c., yet the allegro or adagio may be given with different degrees of quickness, and the designations still be perfectly correct. We have no precise designations for the nicer degrees of tempo, and yet a very slight degree has an influence upon the character of the piece. The metronome, by which in instrumental music the tempo is defined, is only occasionally used as a guide in vocal compositions, because the singer may be guided by the words and by the sentiment which the words indicate.

The *tempi* must be ascertained by a knowledge of the composers, and by reference to the periods in which their compositions first appeared. It would be an error to play an andante by *Bach* or *Haydn* like one of *Chopin's* or *Hiller's*, or sing the allegro of an aria by *Pergolese* or *Caraffa* as quickly as the allegro of one of *Meyerbeer's* arias. But whether a piece of music be light and ornamental in character, or heavy and labored, weak or powerful, quiet or passionate, depends on rhythm and tempo.

COMPOSITION

Classic art sought as the only aim in its works to represent pure beauty. In the compositions of the old masters regard was had only to the sweetness of melody, and everything was excluded from them that did not fall agreeably upon the ear. But in modern music what is even unfavorable to sensuous pleasure is accepted, and we have accustomed ourselves to a more vigorous and powerful mode of representation, the aim being to excite by sudden contrasts.

In so far as music is to represent the most secret life of the soul, and as in art everything natural, so far as it admits of being idealized and represented, is allowable, this tendency of art in music has its justification. But here, as in everything in which the principles of beauty are concerned, the true limit must not be overstepped. The old masters composed only in consonances, and *Helmholtz* has shown scientifically that consonances alone have an independent right to existence. Dissonances, according to *Helmholtz*, are only permissible as transition points for consonants, having no right of their own to be. Down to *Beethoven* we find dissonances correctly employed by all the old masters. And greater and nobler effects were attained than are possible to our modern musicians with their accumulation of dissonances and sudden contrasts.

With the two composers in whom our modern classic epoch reached its zenith, begins the gradual decline of the art of singing. *Mozart* held it necessary to his musical education to study in Italy the vocal compositions of the old masters, and to make himself thoroughly acquainted with the qualities of the singing voice. Hence the vocal compositions of Mozart will remain beautiful and to be held up as models for all time, for they unite the sweetest and loveliest melody with an appreciation of sentiment the noblest and most ideal.

The giant genius of *Beethoven*, inspired and artistic, found the material developed to perfection by his predecessors, and with overpowering strength forced it to yield itself to his service. His masterworks of composition, in the grandeur of their style, excel everything that had been produced before him. But he has treated the human voice as a subordinate instrument.

Because all that *Beethoven* produced was grand and beautiful, he has been blindly imitated, and it has been wholly forgotten that music has in all times drawn its best nourishment from song, and only by means of song has it risen to its high estate, and that instruments can never reach what is possible to a thoroughly educated human voice.

A musician, exclusively devoted to the piano, never dreams of writing a concert piece for the violin, because he knows that he is not sufficiently acquainted with the peculiarities of that instrument; but every musician imagines himself able to compose for the human voice, although its peculiar qualities are far more numerous and far more difficult to be rightly dealt with.

The strictly classical musicians of the present reject all Italian music as bad. The objection made to it is, that the music is never adapted to the words, but often expresses something wholly different and sometimes directly opposite to their meaning, and that it never gives back to us any high, poetic sentiment, but aims to bribe us with ornaments only, and accidents. In regard to modern Italian music this judgment may be just. These superficial compositions are a product of Italian music in its decline, and can force for themselves a certain popularity only by their pleasant and easy melodies. Even the old Italian music seems at first sight to pay little or no regard to the sense of the words, especially when the time, according to the classic German method, is set too quick. Upon closer study, however, we soon perceive that, although the music is treated as the chief thing, the meaning of the words is certainly given when the music is rightly performed. Were it not so, our music would hardly ever have been able to form and develop itself upon and through these old vocal compositions.

As the pictures of Titian, Rubens, and other great painters of that time, who were masters of form as well as of color, will always be considered as works of art and models, so the compositions of the old Italian singing masters and of those who went from their schools are to be held up as examples for vocal composition. In their works, as in all the works of art of that time, form takes precedence of the spirit, that is, the words and their poetic significance are treated as secondary matters. But all the peculiar properties of the human voice find therein due consideration; everything at variance with them is avoided, and every interval, every vowel, is so introduced that the voice can flow out with the greatest perfection. These ornamented compositions can be sung more easily and with less effort than a simple aria of a modern composer.

The fine tact and the correct feeling with which in those old vocal compositions what nature directs was observed, show that they are the works of singers of the golden age of the art of singing, of artists who with an exact knowledge of the beauties and capabilities of the voice possessed, and in those days were compelled to possess, the most thorough culture in the theory of music.

In opposition to this old, classic Italian style of composing song, which considered and treated music for its own sake alone, and regarded the words only in so far as they aided the voice and the expression of the music, stands the classic style of Germany. In this latter the first attention is paid to the poetic meaning and expression of the text. Rightly to apprehend the sense of the words and to give it, by means of the music, a deeper, nobler expression—to transfigure it, as it were—is, according to this style, the purpose of the composer, who commonly has only the slightest reference to the peculiar qualities of the voice and the fitness of the composition to be sung. In the classic Italian style the form predominates—in the German, the inspiration or soul of the composition. In the Italian the music and the singing capability of the composition are attended to almost exclusively. In the German, the main thing is the poetical expression of the signification of the words. When we now sing the wonderful and exquisite compositions of *Schubert, Schumann, Mendelssohn*, etc., we soon feel the impossibility of giving one or another tone as beautifully as it should be given according to the quality of the voice, and as we are able to give it by itself. Or it is hard for us to strike this or that tone with perfect purity or with the requisite force, &c. These songs are *not* adapted to the voice as the old Italian arias were, but composed without accurate knowledge of the voice, and therefore cannot develop the voice in its highest perfection. *Mendelssohn* often lays the strongest

expression in his soprano songs upon the $f^{\sharp 2}$, the transition tone from the falsetto register to the head voice. For the expression of the highest passion, which requires strength, the head voice is not adapted, at least not in its transition tone. Accordingly, it is usually sought to sound this tone with the falsetto register, to which it is not natural, and is therefore hard to be sung, and also becomes sharp and offensive in the male voice especially, where this note is formed just upon the transition from the second chest register into the falsetto. *Schubert*, again, in his songs commonly so places the words that the favorable vowels seldom come upon the right tones. *Schumann* also very often uses intervals which come upon the boundary tones of the register, and can hardly be struck with purity. Thus there are very many hindrances to a fine development of the voice, oftentimes in the most beautiful compositions of our times, hindrances, which many of our composers are more or less chargeable with putting in the way.

It is evident from what has been said that it is by no means a matter of indifference how the words of a song are translated into another language. Compositions easily sung naturally lose by translation, for it is generally left entirely to chance whether the appropriate vowels fall upon the right tones. A teacher must take great care, especially in beginning instruction, to give his pupils compositions adapted to singing. All the exercises and solfeggi should be expressly arranged for the purpose, and also so arranged that the pupil shall have steadily increasing difficulties to encounter, in order that the vocal *technique* may be fully illustrated. Along with these exercises and solfeggi, arias should be practised, particularly at the beginning. The older Italian compositions are the best adapted to vocal culture, because they were made with special reference to the qualities of the voice. Arias are preferable to songs, because they usually require more flexibility of voice, and therefore assist the *technique*. In arias the music is more prominent than in ballads, and the sentiment more marked and consequently more easily apprehended. The same words are commonly more often repeated, and must, of course, be sung differently, and thus the pupil is brought acquainted at once with the different external aids to a fine execution.

EXTERNAL AIDS TO A FINE EXECUTION

A teacher must see to it at first with the utmost attention that all the tones according to their pitch are struck with purity, and this can be done only by his repeating them over and over again to his pupil, because, as we have already remarked, our pianos, according to the present method of tuning, are never sufficiently pure to form a singing tone. When the learner has once become familiarized to the fine sound of pure tones, he will hear and distinguish them, and learn to strike them correctly with our pianos. How important to a fine timbre of the tones the right direction of the breath is and its control, as well as the best mode of securing these points, we have already described at some length. The old Italian masters had established distinct rules by which the breath was to be renewed.

These were:

1. Before the beginning of a phrase.

2. Before trills and passages (*fiorituri*).

3. After tied notes:

4. Before syncopes, and especially accented notes:

5. Between two notes of the same pitch and the same value:

 , in slow phrases.

6. After a short (*staccato*) note:

7. At all pauses and resting-points.

8. Before a note, which, by being accented, was to be especially distinguished in the middle of musical passages, usually before the highest note of a musical phrase, in order to give the music a light, graceful character:

In light, airy pieces of music, this last mode of taking breath had a charming effect, but was mostly left to the taste of the singer. The earlier singers, moreover, were very skilful in finding those places where, according to the character of the composition, an unusual taking of breath was of special effect. On the other hand, it was considered an advantage in a singer to take breath as rarely as possible, and, as we have intimated in the introduction of this book, it was esteemed a great accomplishment to sing long with one inhalation.

In the old Italian music, by which the vocal *technique* is best illustrated, these rules must be observed. In German music the breathing is governed by æsthetic principles, and is regulated by the words of the song. Accordingly, breath can be taken only at the beginning or end of a sentence, conformably to the punctuation. But if the sentences are too long, then the breath is to be taken at some fitting place in the middle of the sentence, so that a word must not be broken by the breath, nor the article or adjective separated from the subject.

An Italian aria, in which the attention is given chiefly to the music and its externals, is executed far more easily and beautifully than a German aria or a German song. Our German ballads, full of deep sentiment and in which the music should give a higher and richer expression to the poetic significance of the words, require in their execution such sterling spiritual culture as only the most extraordinary talent can supply the place of. In the execution of these songs it is, above all things, necessary that the words should be distinctly heard. It easily happens in singing that the noise (*Geräusch*) of the consonants partly from the stronger sound of the tones is entirely covered, and so words are indistinctly heard. The sound of the consonants must, therefore, be given more prominently in singing than in common speech, so that they may be heard along with the tones. It is a good practice to repeat the words, exaggerating the articulation. Thus, by persevering attention, a distinct articulation in singing may be attained without difficulty. Recitative offers an excellent practice for this purpose, the music here being subordinate to the words, according to the intervals of which the composition is for the most part constructed. Although our recitative is formed after the declamation of the Greeks, yet it is not to be sung like this, with pathos, but according to our modern taste, as naturally as possible, just as in a like situation the words would be spoken.[19]

To the external aids to expression belongs the swelling of the tones, one of the easiest, most natural, and most graceful of all our helps. It consists in giving a tone, whose time permits it, different degrees of strength. In a contrary way much time is usually spent in singing the scales, beginning *piano* and increasing in strength to the greatest possible *forte*, and then letting the voice grow weaker and weaker. Instead of these exercises, which require exertion, the same thing can be attained far more easily by swelling the tones where it is required in the composition. In melancholy or mournful compositions, swelling upon those tones which the rhythm requires to be accented is very beautiful. But when exaggerated, or where a fresh, cheerful character is to be preserved in the composition, this aid to expression easily renders the effect sentimental. Unhappily, our whole music is vitiated by this sickly sentimentalism, the perfect horror of every person of cultivated taste. In these later years the powerful reaction of German æsthetics has had favorable results in regard to instrumental music, but in the execution of vocal music this unhealthy fashion of singing still always commands great applause. This sickly sentimental style has also naturalized in singing a gross trick unfortunately very prevalent, the *tremolo* of the notes. When, in rare cases, the greatest passion is to be expressed, to endeavor to deepen the expression by a trembling of the notes is all very well and fully to be justified, but in songs and arias, in which quiet and elevated sentiments are to be expressed, to tremble as if the whole soul were in an uproar, and not at all in a condition for quiet singing, is unnatural and offensive.

A very beautiful aid to expression, but now only seldom heard, is the transition from one register to another on the same note. A note begins with

tolerable strength, for example, *d:*   , with the action belonging to it of the chest register, and while it grows weaker it passes imperceptibly into the action of the falsetto tones. Or the reverse. A note of the chest register is begun with the action of the falsetto, and becoming stronger changes into the chest register to which it naturally belongs. Correctly employed, the most delightful effects may be produced in this way, especially by a male voice.

Ornaments, such as *appoggiaturas* and *turns, roulades, trills,* &c., are to be used only with taste and care. The old Italian compositions, which were so arranged as to show the voice in its fullest brilliancy, have their ornaments commonly in such phrases as were to be first sung several times in a simpler way. In the frequent repetition of the same melody and words, those places

were designated by so-called *firmates,* thus: , where it was permitted to the artist to introduce embellishments according to his own taste. In German arias embellishments are allowed to be introduced according to the taste of the singer, only, however, with the greatest care; but in German ballads not at all. And yet we often hear artists, who have acquired a certain flexibility of voice, introducing their little trickeries in the most inappropriate places.

But none of these aids to expression are to be used so often as to become mere mannerisms. Only when employed in due measure can they have an æsthetically fine effect. As so much depends upon the taste of the singer, it is necessary that he should, above all things, have a thorough appreciation of the sentiment which is to find expression in the piece, and seek to make it his own, and then the ornament is to be introduced only where it accords with the sentiment, that is, where it is appropriate. The two greatest artists of the present day, Lind and Stockhausen, whose expression is perfect, take great pains to understand the composition thoroughly, and in this way to be fully imbued with the sentiment.

Without the animation of a soul, singing fails of all effect upon the hearer, and is ordinary and wearisome. But this animation must be with understanding and taste—i. e., æsthetically beautiful. For the beautiful continues beautiful and true only as long as it is in proportion and not exaggerated—only while those fine lines are not transgressed where it begins to be untrue, that is, affected and ridiculous.

TIME OF INSTRUCTION

The old Italians began with quite young pupils, commonly when they were in their ninth or tenth year. The great demands which were then made in regard to the technical culture of the voice required a long time for instruction, usually five or six years. The extraordinary fulness and power of tone possessed by the earlier artists could be acquired only by persevering and adequate practice of the vocal organ, taken while in the process of growth. Those singers, men and women, whose voices have been celebrated for their fulness and strength of tone, such as *Catalani, Perini,* &c., sang in their fifth year, under the careful oversight of persons musically cultivated. In childhood the impulse to imitation is strongest, the vocal organs are more tender and pliant than in adults; and hence, when care is taken to avoid fatiguing and straining the voice, children learn much easier and better than grown persons. They are also preserved by early and correct singing from the many bad habits with which the teacher has to contend in adults. That special skill and care are required in a teacher who has in charge the voices of children, there can be no question. But unhappily, no regard is paid to this consideration in the system of teaching singing in the schools, universally introduced in France, Germany, and Switzerland. To any teacher who can sing at all, or play on any instrument, the tender voices of children are entrusted, and he allows them to sing together in chorus, satisfied if the tones are not grossly false and the time is kept, paying no regard to the formation of the voice. Now it is well known that even practised singers avoid singing much in chorus, considering it injurious to the voice. Although schooled and educated voices can endure a much greater strain than children's voices, yet children are often, without any understanding, required to sing loud, in order "to bring out the voice." In such a way of singing it is simply impossible that every separate voice should be attended to, even were the teacher competent to attend to it; while it often happens that at the most critical age, while the vocal organs are being developed, children sing with all the strength they can command. Boys, however, in whom the larynx at a certain period undergoes an entire transformation, reach only with difficulty the higher soprano or contralto tones, but are not assigned a lower part until, perceiving themselves the impossibility of singing in this way, they beg the teacher for the change, often too late, unhappily, to prevent an irreparable injury. Moderate singing, without exertion, and, above all things, within the natural limits of the voice and its registers, would even during the period of growth be as little hurtful as speaking, laughing, or any other of the exercises which cannot be forbidden to the vocal organs. But it is wiser not to allow boys to sing at all while the larynx is undergoing its change.

The plan of introducing into schools instruction in singing, so excellent in itself theoretically, tends, by the way in which it is carried out in practice, to lessen the number of voices susceptible of artistic culture, without any compensation in an awakened feeling and understanding of music. In the palmy days of the art of singing there was no instruction given in singing in the schools, but there were instead numerous schools for singing, where children were trained into artists by the most skilful teachers, and whence proceeded good singers, male and female, in great numbers.

The numerous vocal music Unions and *Männerchöre*, as such, contribute as little as school singing to the elevation and improvement of the vocal art, the sole object of which is to cultivate the individual voice for artistic singing. Considered as a means of moral culture, the rise and increasing prevalence of chorus singing among all orders of the people merit commendation and aid, but not in the interest of the art of song.

Apart from this school instruction, now becoming so popular, people commonly venture to entrust their sons and daughters, but not until they are quite grown, to a singing master to be educated. But then it is expected that he shall, in the shortest time possible, often in the space of a few months, advance them so far that they shall be able to sing with applause before company.

Such is the case in Germany, and in a much higher degree in America, while in the various conservatories of Europe there is now required a period of from four to seven years for education in the art of singing. In the Conservatory of Milan, which is now held to be the best school for our art, pupils are admitted only upon the condition that they will remain seven years.

Thus, while every instrument, if anything is to be made out of it, demands years of practice, to the human voice alone is time denied, simply because, I suppose, almost every one has a somewhat natural aptitude for singing.

The greatest fault, however, is to be found in the present mode of teaching singing, which is so superficial that people have become accustomed to overlook the possibility of changing a voice and rendering it beautiful. For the most part instruction begins where and with what it should end; the aim is, paying only passing attention to the timbre and the formation of tone (*Tonbildung*), to teach the pupil to sing certain favorite pieces with the due execution, and to see that the breath is taken at the right places and that the tone is not too impure. But the human voice is susceptible of much higher culture than any instrument. And it requires more gifts and far more study to become a true and distinguished artist in singing than are necessary to the mastery of other instruments. It would most assuredly contribute to the advancement and elevation of the vocal art, if gifted children, as it often happened in former times, were early instructed in singing with the requisite care and skill. Thus, educated for their art, and giving to it their best powers, they would be able to satisfy far higher demands and attain to quite another and higher artistic perfection than we are wont now-a-days to find anywhere among our vocal artists. Such children would then, at the age at which at present instruction in singing begins, have already mastered all technical difficulties and be able to apply themselves chiefly to the æsthetic cultivation of their art. With young girls especially, whose vocal organs do not change so much as those of boys, the earliest possible beginning of instruction would be in the highest degree advantageous. It is owing only to the unnatural, overstrained method of studying the art of singing now prevalent that a principle recognized and applied in the learning of all other arts, and even in all the other branches of music, has universal prejudice against it.

CONCLUSION

An artist can be formed only by his own intelligence and practice, under the direct guidance of a master. But here, more than in any other art, the constant watchfulness of a teacher is a necessity. For, as one gets only an imperfect idea of his own personal appearance from a mirror, so the singer and dramatic artist can form but a partial judgment of his own performances. They are too subjective, and cannot be viewed as an external whole, like the works of the painter and sculptor. It is, moreover, as has already been remarked, simply impossible to obtain even a partial knowledge of any art from books alone, even if we were able to describe with precision the fine, delicate differences of tones, colors and forms.

These pages, therefore, make no claim whatever to be regarded as a manual of singing. They aim only to communicate and extend a knowledge of the latest discoveries and advances in the domain of vocal art, and to protest against and correct prevailing prejudices and errors in regard to this art, as well as to engage the attention of those to whose care the culture of the voice is entrusted.

---

18 The friends of this style of music (programme music so called) appeal to the authority of Beethoven, who, it is claimed, opened the way for it when he introduced into his *Pastoral Symphony* interlineations which should suggest the right sentiment to the hearer. But, although Beethoven allowed himself to approach the uttermost limits in this direction, he never overstepped them. It was only in his *Pastoral Symphony* that he introduced these interlineations, and they do not entirely contradict the peculiar character of the music, as so many of our modern programmes do.

Programme
To Beethoven's Pastoral Symphony, December 22, 1808.

I.Agreeable sensations upon visiting the country.

II.Scene at a brook's side.

III.Merry gathering of country people.

IV.Thunder and storm.

V.Happy and grateful emotions after the storm.
More emotional than descriptive.
Expression rather than representation of feeling.

To a Prize Symphony, by Joachim Raff, performed in Vienna, 1863.

I. D major. Allegro.

Portrait of the German character,—its capability of elevation, proneness to Reflection, Gentleness and Valor, as contrasts that blend with and permeate one another in manifold ways—overpowering proneness to meditation.

II. D minor. Allegro molto vivace.

In the open air, in the German grove, with the sound of horns, Away to the fields, with the songs of the people.

III. D major. Larghetto.

Gathering round the domestic hearth, transfigured by love and the Muses.

IV. G minor. Allegro-dramatico.

Ineffectual struggle to establish the unity of the fatherland.

V. D minor. Lament. D major. Allegro trionfale.

Opening of a new and elevated era.

---

19 Although our recitative is formed after the recitative of the ancient drama, yet the latter, according to all accounts, appears to have been very different from our opera recitative, and to have had greater resemblance to the monotonous recitation of the Romish Liturgy, which seems to be a relic of ancient art.

APPENDIX

STRUCTURE OF THE VOCAL ORGANS

THE larynx is a sound-giving organ belonging to that class of wind instruments called reed instruments, although it differs in various respects from all artificial arrangements of the kind. The sound or tone-generating apparatus of the larynx consists of tense, elastic *membranes*, the so-called *chordæ vocales*, which are enclosed in a sounding case composed of movable cartilaginous plates, and may be stretched by a certain apparatus of muscles in very different and exactly measurable degrees. They are made to vibrate audibly by a current of air impelled with various degrees of force and at will by the lungs in expiration through the narrow chink (glottis) formed by the fine edges of the chords. Thus the lungs correspond to the bellows of the organ; the trachea, at the top of which the vocal instrument is placed, answers to the conduit (*Windrohr*), and the cavity of the throat in front of the instrument with its two avenues, the mouth and the nostrils, to the resonance pipe (*Ansatzrohr*).

THE LUNGS

The lungs are two cellular, sponge-like elastic organs, largely made up of little cavities of conical shape, which, in the regular alternations of two opposite respiratory movements of air, are at one time expanded, and then again compressed. The two lungs are not of equal size; the right lung is one-tenth larger in volume than the left.

THE TRACHEA, OR WINDPIPE,

Through which the air of the lungs enters and passes out, consists of from sixteen to twenty-six cartilaginous rings, posteriorly incomplete, lying horizontally one above the other.

These rings are connected by a membrane covering them externally and internally. As they enter the cavity of the chest, they divide into two branches, likewise composed of rings, one entering the right, the other the left lung. Before they join the lungs they divide again into several smaller branches, which again subdivide fork-like in the lungs, and terminate in numberless little grape-like clusters of hollow vesicles. The diameter of the trachea in adults is from one-half to three-fourths of an inch when at rest.

THE LARYNX

The larynx may be regarded as the funnel-shaped termination of the trachea. It enlarges upward and is composed of various cartilages more or less mobile, connected by ligaments and moved by muscles. The exterior of the larynx is formed by the

I.Thyroid cartilage.

II.Cricoid cartilage.

The cartilages in the interior are:

I.The Arytenoid cartilages.

II.Cartilages of Wrisberg.

III.Cartilages of Santorini.

IV.Cuneiform cartilages.

To the cartilages of the larynx must be further added the Epiglottis, with the little cartilage at the centre of its inner side.

1. The *thyroid cartilage* is the largest cartilage of the larynx, and consists of two four-cornered cartilaginous plates held together in front and diverging behind; the anterior borders are convex, and consequently where the two plates meet in front they form an upper and a lower notch or slit. The posterior angles of this cartilage extend into the so-called horns of the *thyroid cartilage*. At the upper horns are ligaments attached, which form the connection between the hyoid bone and the larynx, while the lower horns serve to join the thyroid to the cricoid cartilage. In females and boys the angle formed by the two plates of the *thyroid cartilage* is obtuse. In the male sex at a certain period the larynx changes its shape, and the plates of the *thyroid cartilage* then form an acute angle, which is visible on the outside of the throat, and is popularly known as the *Adam's apple*. At this time the diameter of the male larynx becomes a third larger than that of the female larynx, and in consequence the voice is lower, and its different registers are more enlarged in compass.

2. The *cricoid cartilage* resembles in shape a seal ring; its broader side is situated posteriorly between the lower horns of the *thyroid cartilage*, and it is connected by its lower edges immediately with the upper edge of the first ring of the trachea. From its side at the back part project two rounded surfaces, which give attachment to the *arytenoid cartilages*.

3. The *arytenoid cartilages* are two small but very mobile bodies in the form of three-cornered pyramids. The base of the pyramid rests upon the before-mentioned rounded surface at the back of the upper border of the *cricoid cartilage*; one of its sides turns to the front, the two others to the back and outwards. The surfaces between the anterior and postero-interior corners are accordingly turned towards one another. The surface posteriorly is concave, and affords space for a part of the *arytenoid muscle*; the inner surface is smooth, and forms, during quiet breathing, a part of the lateral wall of the larynx; the anterior surface is rough and irregular, and to it adhere the *vocal chords*, the

thyro-arytenoid muscle, the *lateral and posterior crico-arytenoid muscles*, and upon these the bases of the *cuneiform cartilages*. The *arytenoid cartilages* are lengthened at their summits by two little pear-shaped elevations, the *cartilages of Santorini* (called *apophyses* in Garcia's observations), which are connected with them by ligamentous fibres, and extend with them some distance into the larynx.

4. The *cartilages of Wrisberg* are described by Hyrtl as slight elevations upon the front or anterior edge of the *arytenoid cartilages*, inclining towards the interior, and, like all parts of the larynx, covered by the mucous membrane.

5. The *cuneiform cartilages* (as Wilson names them) are two long, slender cartilaginous laminæ which become somewhat broader at both ends. These cartilages, with their base, rest in the middle of the anterior surface of the *arytenoid cartilages*, and reach to the middle of the vocal chords, by which they are enveloped. The action of these cartilages renders possible the production of the head tones, but they are not found in every larynx. The fact that they are oftener found in the female larynx than in that of the male, and that the male larynx is mostly used in scientific investigations, as it is larger and more easily dissected, may be the reason why up to the present time no mention is made of them either in German or French manuals. They are sometimes referred to as cuneiform cartilages, or confounded with the cartilages of Wrisberg, probably because it seemed unaccountable that these important bodies should so long have escaped the attention of anatomists.

From the anterior surface of the *arytenoid cartilages*, extending towards the centre of the inner wall of the *thyroid cartilage*, running diagonally through the cavity of the larynx, are stretched the two pairs of chords already more than once mentioned—the vocal chords, consisting of folds of the mucous membrane which envelopes the whole larynx. The two lower of these chords, the vocal chords strictly so called, into which the *cuneiform cartilages* project and through which the interior thyro-arytenoid muscles run, have their points of attachment at the *arytenoid cartilages*, somewhat lower than the upper pair. Each of these parallel pairs of chords form between their lips a slit running antero-posteriorly. The slit of the upper pair is opened in the shape of an ellipse; that of the lower pair, the glottis, is very narrow. As the upper chords have their point of attachment posteriorly and higher, they form with the lower chords two lateral cavities, the ventricles.

The two pairs of chords, therefore, are the free interior edges of the membrane, covering the whole larynx and extending into it to the right and the left. Only the lower vocal chords serve directly for the generation of tones. More or less stretched and presenting resistance to the air forcibly expired from the lungs through the trachea, they are thus made to vibrate. The upper or false vocal chords do not co-operate with them to generate tone, but like all the remaining parts of the mouth and throat belong to the resonance apparatus of the voice, to which also appertains the back part of the mouth, the *pharynx*, over the œsophagus, the throat, or gullet. This is separated from the anterior cavity of the mouth by the palate, which is a curtain formed by the mucous membranes of the cavity of the mouth, and the centre of which forms the pendent uvula.

Above the œsophagus, immediately over the palate, lie close together, and separated only by a very thin osseous partition, the two posterior nasal orifices. These serve as passages for the air during inspiration and expiration; they are likewise considered as belonging to the resonance apparatus.

Upon both sides of the cavity of the mouth, between the two wings of the palate, lie the tonsils, two glandular bodies, which separate the sides of the cavity of the mouth from the *pharynx*. The anterior cavity of the mouth, which is separated from the nasal cavities by the palate, requires no description, as every one can acquaint himself with its structure in his own person and in others. Upon its formation, as well as upon the position of its different parts and upon the character of those parts of the larynx and of the cavity of the mouth which have been described as the resonance apparatus, the difference in the fulness and timbre of tones depends.

The *epiglottis* is fixed at the anterior portion of the larynx, at the root of the tongue, within the angle formed by the two surfaces of the thyroid cartilage. It is a very elastic fibro-cartilage, freely moving in a posterior direction. Its color is yellowish and its general form that of a spoon; its upper surface is covered with a multitude of little mucous glands set in shallow cavities. In the downward passage of food the *epiglottis* covers the upper orifice of the larynx like a valve, over which the food passes into the œsophagus or gullet, without being able to enter the larynx and the trachea. In the centre of its interior side there is a little rounded cartilage, movable in every direction, which has as yet no name. Czermak mentions it first in his observations with the laryngoscope. In the male larynx, after the voice has altered, the cartilages become more or less ossified and gradually harden with increasing age. The cartilages of the female larynx, with rare exceptions, usually continue with little or no change. The muscles, by which the movements of the larynx are effected, are:

I.The posterior crico-arytenoid.

II.The lateral crico-arytenoid.

III.The crico-arytenoid.

IV.The thyro-arytenoid.

V.The arytenoid.

VI.The internal thyro-arytenoid.

In late works upon laryngoscopy the different muscles of the larynx are variously designated and divided. Bataille terms the first three of the above-named muscles the exterior muscles of the larynx; the three others he comprehends under the name of thyro-arytenoid or vocal muscle, which divides into three slips in the interior of the larynx. This, however, as well as the description of the character and action of the different muscles, belongs to the department of science. What I have already stated seems to me to be sufficient for an understanding of the action of these organs in the production of sound in the different registers. The reader is referred to any good manual of anatomy for a full description of the muscles, ligaments, nerves, vessels and membranes.

THE END.

9 789362 995667